CHANNELLING:

THE SPIRITUAL CONNECTION

A Balanced Perspective

Zoë Hagon

PRISM
PRESS

Originally published in 1988 in Australia by Equinox Publishing

This revised edition published in Great Britain in 1989 by

PRISM PRESS
2 South Street
Bridport
Dorset DT6 3NQ

and distributed in the USA by

AVERY PUBLISHING GROUP INC.
350 Thorens Avenue
Garden City Park
New York 11040

ISBN 1 85327 043 1

Reprinted 1990

Printed and bound in the Channel Islands
by The Guernsey Press Company Limited.

Acknowledgements

Special thanks are due to Gael Walker for her assistance with the manuscript; to Lis Moller and Andrew Watson for helping me to overcome the fear; to Malcom for starting me off on the road so many years ago; to Kirsten for her understanding and acceptance of all the times I couldn't be with her due to writing this book; and thanks to all those who appear in this book for the time and patience which they so generously gave me.

This book is dedicated to Libby, with thanks for the constant support, caring and encouragement.

CONTENTS

Chapter One

What is Channelling?

Over the last decade there has been a huge explosion in the growth movement across the world. Everywhere people are attending workshops, seminars and conferences, trying to become aware of themselves as more than just physical beings. As there has been an increase in this awareness, people are becoming more understanding of their wholeness — of being a subtle balance of body, mind and spirit. As part of this trend, many have become conscious of their inherent spirituality. One of the results of this is a marked expansion of what is termed channelling.

What is this current upsurge in channelling all about? Why have such a wide variety of channels suddenly emerged on the world scene and what is it about these so-called channels that seems to draw people to them like iron filings to a magnet? Why is it that some people are prepared to give up responsibility for themselves and listen only to what the channel says?

These and other questions are frequently being asked by bewildered and often sceptical members of the community at large, and I will endeavour to answer them in the course of this chapter.

So, what actually is a channel in this sense? In physical terms, a channel is a route through which anything passes or progresses; to channel something is to direct it towards a particular course. Similarly, in the psychic or spiritual sense, a channel is someone who is able to transmit psychic or spiritual energy into our physical reality. It is someone who is sufficiently able to bypass their intellect and/or ego, in order to allow this energy through. In other words, channels are people who have learnt to get themselves — their conscious minds — out of the way in order to bring through information, healing and so on from another dimension or reality into our physical world.

This channelling comes from a variety of sources and may be available for many different reasons. Often it is intended for the individual alone, but information may also come through specifically to be communicated to the world at large. It can take a wide range of forms, all of which I intend to cover in this book, but for now, I will briefly run through the different types of channelling existing throughout the world, and how some of them are utilised.

Channelling usually takes place while the receiver is in either a meditative or a trance (unconscious) state; in other words, while the conscious mind is relaxed. It is as simple as 'the still, small, voice within', and many people, often unknowingly, tune into this on a regular basis. They listen to their intuition, their inner feelings, their gut reaction, and act accordingly.

To me, channelling seems to come from four main sources: the Higher Self, or the superconscious within; the God Energy; the universal or collective unconscious; or spirit beings from another plane of consciousness, sometimes known as guides, masters and so on.

The purpose of channelling may be purely for the benefit of the person concerned: a way of that person tuning in to his or her own inner guidance, which is strictly for him or her at that time. It may also come through in order to help others in the form of information, as spiritual healing (as in the laying on of hands), or for the release of earthbound spirits. It may be wide-scale information that is to be printed in the form of a book, for example *The Course in Miracles* or *Seth Speaks*, or it may come through as a teaching, such as the information transmitted by well-known spirit entities such as White Eagle, Silver Birch, or currently Ramtha and Lazaris. Some channelling may come through in the form of a message from Great Uncle Fred who died last year and wants to communicate with those he left behind, and some may be in the form of music, poetry or art, such as in paintings of dead relatives, spirit guides or message paintings.

However, what is really important, regardless of the source, is that ANYONE can be a channel for their own inner wisdom: anyone can go within and tune into their own inner wisdom. Ken Carey, author of the channelled *Starseed Transmissions*, in a talk to the Findhorn Foundation in 1986, said that 'everyone of us is capable of blending our individual consciousness with the universal consciousness of the Creator'; and certainly, over the past few years, more and more people have begun to accept responsibility for their own lives, and to understand the process of tuning into themselves on a deeper level.

In the past the term 'channelling' was never used. The word was 'mediumship', and this word itself was enough to frighten people away. This was mainly due to connotations of little old ladies working behind the closed doors of a Victorian drawing room in order to contact spirits. These mediums were mainly channelling information from the spirit of someone who had died and wanted to make contact with a loved one left behind. The mediums would also channel guides (a group of souls who are said to be with each person throughout his/her physical life in order to provide help and guidance), either their own, or ones belonging to the person searching.

Over the years the role of the medium seems to have expanded out of a very private domain and into public life. Now channelling is given to public audiences, sometimes to hundreds at a time, when previously it would have been appropriate only in spiritualist churches. Some of these public audiences have been televised, and many are now available on video for people to view in the comfort of their own homes as often as they choose.

In the past channelling was surrounded by a sense of withdrawal and intrigue, and there was a strong belief that mediums were somehow special and even enlightened. This is not so: in fact, in the past many psychics, especially those doing psychic readings as opposed to specific channelling, were anything but enlightened. What they were doing was using their quite considerable mind power to harness the universal energy or collective unconscious: a function of a part of the brain that would have either spontaneously developed or could have been trained to bring about certain changes by power of the will.

For example, it is power of the mind that enables a psychic to levitate, to bend spoons, move objects, use telepathy (mind-to-mind communication) or tune in to the higher or psychic senses. In fact these senses, whether we are conscious of them or not, are with us all the time. However we are not trained to recognise and use them, and very often we are taught to deny or distrust their existence. But if we can acknowledge the age-old philosophies that describe man as a dual being, and can accept that as well as having a physical body and mind, we also have a spirit body and mind — what many term the soul aspect — then these higher or psychic senses are more understandable. They relate exactly to the five physical senses, but on a non-physical level, with the commonest being clairvoyance, clairaudience and clairsentience.

Clairvoyance, or clear seeing, is the ability to perceive people, events and objects outside of one's immediate environment and without using the physical sense of sight: for example, when a psychic sees a spirit with a person, or sees the aura surrounding that person. Clairaudience is the ability of a person to hear voices or sounds which are beyond the range of the normal physical sense of hearing. For example, a friend of mine heard me warning him to take an important case out of his car — and in fact his car was broken into during the following hour! Clairsentience is the ability to sense beyond the limits of our immediate physical surroundings, and beyond our three-dimensional reality. It is possessed by those people who can walk into a house and immediately sense a presence there. The higher senses of taste and smell may also exist in such situations, but they are far less common. These are all abilities that develop through the mind.

Unfortunately, it is also through mind control that various non-acceptable practices take place: there are instances of unscrupulous, so-called gurus who teach their students to take control of another person's mind, and to coerce that person into performing some specific task. Control of another person's mind still takes place in society today: apart from brain-washing techniques that have been well researched and documented, there are also incidents of hexes or curses being put on people — with or without their knowledge — sometimes in more primitive societies, but also in modern Western countries.

However there is one important factor to bear in mind: energy itself is benign. It is neither good nor bad. It is how it is utilised that is the key. The same energy that can be used to heal and cure can be harnessed to injure or kill. It is totally up to the person concerned.

Channelling consists of bringing this energy from another level through to our physical reality. The channelling I am referring to is the kind that I term, 'broad spectrum channelling'. It is not just information received from a non-physical entity or spirit as is the accepted definition, but it also encompasses energy from all the different sources I mentioned earlier, and can be used for healing, wisdom, the arts, and much more. It can be practical in its application and very down-to-earth and even humorous. For example, a woman I know regularly tunes in to her inner guidance when she wants a new recipe to cook for her family!

However, the 'norm', if there is one, is for the channelling of spiritual energy to encourage or help people in their search for spiritual inner wisdom, enlightenment, and healing on a deep inner level. In order to do this properly it is important that the channel is as clear and open as possible. Just as a poor quality radio picks up a lot of static and distortion, so a 'poor quality' channel will obviously not receive and transmit as clear and pure a form of energy or information as that received and transmitted by a good channel. So what is it that makes a clear channel?

For a start, the relative purity of the channel's own life will attract energy on the same level through the law of resonance. This means that someone who is self-centred, fearful, full of anger, greed etc. will obviously attract similar energy, or a spirit with similar characteristics. The use of drugs and alcohol also tends to distort communication and often attracts lower entities. Someone who is emotionally balanced and centred, whose life is dedicated to helping others, and who is applying the information received to helping others, and who is applying the information received to further his/her own spiritual development, will attract a far higher or clearer energy or spirit. For me, the most important aspect of channels is that they should have a heart centre that is open and flowing — where the energy is transformed into the power of unconditional love, the Christ Consciousness.

The heart centre, or heart *chakra* as it is known in Eastern philosophy, is centred on the sternum at the front of the body, and midway between the shoulder blades on the spine. It is an energy centre, the centre for focusing love — not sexual love, not romantic love, but love that is totally unconditional. It is the centre for giving and receiving this love without any thought of, or need for, return: this is love in its purest essence. It is the centre for impersonal feelings such as trust, compassion, empathy, humility and so on, and is concerned with concepts of the whole, or group consciousness.

Many people have a heart centre with very blocked energy. They may have blocks stemming from childhood issues — from not having received enough love as a baby or child; they may be scared of loving because of pain this has brought in the past; they may have been physically or emotionally abused so that love is not a part of their universal make-up or understanding, and so it goes on.

When I talk of an open heart, I'm referring to people who have released many of their emotional blocks or issues, and often these people, during the process of releasing, have forged a strong spiritual connection — a link with their own Higher Self or Divinity within.

The analogy I sometimes use for easier understanding is that of a vessel containing muddy water: if you pour clear water into the vessel it will stir up the mud that has settled, but the mud will still remain. The water will never become totally clear. However if you flush out the mud, then the clear water can be held and used. So too with channelling spiritual energy: if the vessel or person is still full of mud or emotional 'garbage', then the water or energy coming through will be polluted. Once the garbage is released, then the energy will be pure. All very simple, yet in reality it can take years (or lifetimes) of learning, growing, and releasing this emotional flotsam and jetsam.

It is most important for those channelling spiritual energy that they are as clear as possible, they are not working from their egos, and that they don't fall into the trap of believing that spiritual work means forgetting and denying the physical and all its components in order to rise above reality and become pure and holy. As a healer friend of mine puts it, 'If you become too heavenly, you're no earthly good'. It's a balance that is necessary — we're here in a physical body in order to learn, not to deny its existence, and part of that learning is bringing the spiritual down to this reality and integrating it in our everyday life. We are learning to balance the physical, emotional and spiritual aspects of our nature so that we can grow further towards the ultimate goal of perfection or oneness with all things.

It's all too easy to be off with the pixies, living with our heads in the clouds, and our feet barely touching the ground. But that's not integrating spirituality into our lives. Rather it's an escape into the spiritual, and lovely as that is, it's not very productive.

So, if someone wants to visit a channel, how is it possible to recommend such a person and know that the channel is reliable? First and foremost, I will always suggest that the person turn inward and tune in to their own divinity within to gain the inner wisdom and guidance they are seeking. Nothing can replace the personal relationship to God, the highest spiritual source.

However when people still wish to go ahead and consult a channel, then it's best to look for one who has experienced much personal growth, who has cleared many of his/her own emotional blocks, and who has his/her feet firmly planted on the ground while still being in contact with the higher energies. These people are less likely to be sidetracked by the ego. It's also worth having a look at the channel's own life: ask yourself whether the work is being used to help others and further spiritual awareness, or whether it is only being used as a way of making money to create a more opulent lifestyle?

According to Corinne McLaughlin (co-founder of Sirius Community, a spiritual community in Massachusetts, USA, and co-founder of the School of Spiritual Science there), 'A good test is to ask yourself whether you'd go to this person for spiritual advice if she wasn't channelling. Do you trust this person to be wiser spiritually than yourself, or is it merely "channelling chic" that attracts you to them?'. She continues:

> Unfortunately, what can sometimes happen is that a channel may start out being well-intentioned and sincere in their efforts to help others spiritually and so attract a helpful spirit guide, but then as increasing attention and power come their way, their personality is not pure enough

to handle it. The ego gets inflated and a lesser spirit gets attracted. This second one is a lower entity who may masquerade as the first spirit and start subtly distorting the message and trying to control others through guilt or threats.

Another word of caution: as mentioned earlier, it is always more advisable to go within than to rely on someone else — in going within you find your own truth and not someone else's. However, if you do choose to listen to that offered by someone else, please don't give up responsibility for yourself. Just because a disembodied spirit might tell you something, it doesn't mean it is necessarily right. After all, if you never listened to Uncle Fred when he was alive, why should you presume that everything he says now is full of wisdom and should be acted upon accordingly? The being may be from a higher plane of consciousness, but it may also be from a lower one or even from the channel's own subconscious. You are still in charge of your own life, and the best guide of all is your gut feeling, your intuition, and your own inner guidance. If it feels wrong, then most probably it is.

Whether or not an entity is supposed to be a Master or a Higher Being, only do or act as you FEEL is right and appropriate for you at the time. (I once had a teacher who said that any beings who insisted that you MUST do something should be known as the 'mustabators'. If directions came from that level, then ignore them!) A real Master never demands, but always suggests, and this suggestion is always accompanied by a sense of wisdom and love. After all, he has 'mastered' all levels of existence. A masquerader, of which unfortunately there are many, behaves totally differently. He generally lacks love, and is far more demanding and expectant of his followers.

My rough rule of thumb is the higher the level of the beings, the less likely they are to talk about it. The lower they are, the more they need to brag. If a being is from a really high level, then no-one can mistake the energy in the room at the time. It can be felt and sensed by most people. I am talking here of the channelling of spiritual beings as opposed to just the energy alone. Both are valid forms of channelling, however; neither is right or wrong.

According to Andrew Watson, the South African-born healer, there are basically three main forms of channelling. The first is where people are connecting to what Jung called the collective unconscious. On the whole, the information coming from this level is already known — it is more or less identical from person to person, and although it may well have value in helping individuals in whatever processes they are going through, it no longer has value for the whole. The second form is concerned with contacting the internal and creative Higher Self, which is where Watson feels most people are channelling from. This can bring through new ideas and new creations in consciousness from the higher aspects. The third form he cites is where the channelling is coming from 'The Gods of the Past' — past masters, gurus and world teachers — although he's not totally convinced that even they are bringing together new material, as some of the predictions made recently were in fact also made long ago by people such as Nostradamus.

Andrew Watson also feels that many of the fears in the collective unconscious can be merely reflected back through the channel, and people mistake it for the truth simply because it came from the channel. Many people then rush out in a state of panic and do things they normally would never dream of — things they certainly would not have done if they had been centred and in touch with their true essence within.

The most important aspect of this whole subject of channelling is the desire and the ability to go within — to know who we really are, not to think of ourselves in a particular role (usually associated with job or family) but to find that 'still, small voice' within ourselves where we can actually begin to get a sense of who we are and why we're here and where we belong in the pattern of life. It is a matter of finding the silence within which we can listen and begin to hear and see what really is.

The question now arises as to why channelling has suddenly become fashionable. What is it about channelled messages that have such a popular appeal and why is the word 'spiritual' coming out of organised religion and into everyday life and living?

One explanation may be the democratic nature of the

phenomenon — the fact that anyone can channel messages from another level. Many people who have recently achieved fame and fortune started out as housewives, businessmen and so on; they didn't spend years of training and deprivation in order to unveil their gift, as would have been the case in the past. Another reason for the recent popularity of channelling could well be the fact that many channels tell people what their egos want to hear. For example, 'You're perfect just as you are' or 'You can achieve whatever you want' and so on.

Some people seem to find it easier to accept advice from a non-physical entity who doesn't instil the fear associated with most authority figures; and still others may be lured by the fact that the rich and famous have made much of channelling. For example, Shirley MacLaine and other movie stars have written about their experiences, and have been seen on television listening to the words of wisdom from their particular disembodied guru, and now run workshops to do with the teachings from these various channels. In the tele-movie *Out on a Limb*, which starred Shirley MacLaine as herself, scenes were shown of trance channelling actually taking place. The two channels concerned played themselves and were filmed as they went into trance and then allowed their respective spirit beings to talk through them.

However this doesn't really answer the question as to why channelling has emerged so strongly at this time. We are currently in the so-called New Age, and many people see this as the awakening of a single universal intelligence in our midst, a process we are currently experiencing as a global human family. We are beginning a time of transition — from the Piscean Age into the Aquarian Age — and many believe this is specifically concerned with offering healing into the collective unconscious, and so to the planet as a whole. It is a time in which the individual learns to take responsibility for him or herself, and yet chooses to create a collective force which, through its own energy, will bring about change.

There is an intensity of love energy at this time, but also an intensification of fear energy, and these often overlap, causing conflict. However if we can change the fear by bringing it into conscious understanding, and instead of converting it into violence or suicide, we can love it and heal it, then it can be released.

It seems as if the Age of Aquarius is the time for people to stop hiding behind the illusions they have created down through the centuries, and to open up to reality, to the truth within, and to start truly being themselves.

According to some mystics and psychics, now is the time that many people who lived in Atlantis are returning — to use their gifts this time round for the betterment of mankind, instead of for destruction. This is their explanation for the recent upsurge of interest in spiritual matters. According to *Time* (Australia) magazine: 'The New Age is a combination of spirituality and superstition, fad and farce, about which the only thing certain is that it is not new'. Nobody seems to know where it has sprung from, or even why it has started, but it's obviously here to stay, for some time at any rate, with all its trappings, both good and not so good.

Many people have written and spoken of the significance of this Age of Aquarius, and in almost every language writings are to be found which predict what is going to happen to this planet, and humanity, during the next few decades. From the Relevations of St John the Divine, through Nostradamus to Edgar Cayce, one can discover many predictions which all point to the fact that the years leading toward the end of the century will be exceptionally critical in the earth's evolutionary process.

As the world has seen an increase in both violence and disease, it is as if we are witnessing the symptoms of a fatal disease in modern Western society. Many people are finding they just cannot cope with life, and yet many others are beginning to seek understanding of themselves and their purpose in society. In recent years more and more people have begun to recognise and to use more than just their five physical senses. They are becoming aware of levels of existence beyond themselves, beyond their physical selves. To many it's as if a veil has been lifted and they can become aware of a source of knowledge and wisdom which can best be described as universal or infinite consciousness.

There are many people throughout the world who are in contact with this universal consciousness. Many channels of communication have been established, especially over the last twenty years or so, and from these it appears that many believe that they are here to act as channels for the release of 'new' knowledge. These people feel a strong guiding force in their lives leading them along a sometimes lonely, yet fulfilling, path. Like attracts like, and to these channels come those who intuitively feel that the wisdom displayed truly reflects this universal consciousness.

Apart from significant astrological changes currently taking place (these are seen to occur every 2000 years), another reason some authorities give for this recent upsurge in spiritual awareness is the occurrence of changes in the subtle life-force body of the earth. Apparently this planetary 'etheric web' has been torn apart due to wars and atomic explosions, and without this protection there is a much greater influx of psychic energy which makes communication with non-physical realities easier and more feasible.

One point we need to remember is that channelling is not exclusively a 'New Age' phenomenon. Although it's become relatively acceptable in many societies today, and no longer will one be tortured or killed for acknowledging communion with spirits and the like, many ethnic cultures have always had individuals or even groups who have claimed to have received messages or information from beyond the earth plane. For example, many of the Aboriginal shamans and witchdoctors in various primitive societies have been channelling spirits as part of their cultural heritage in both ceremonial rituals and healing rites since time immemorial. This was totally acceptable by the societies concerned, and it seems as if only the so-called civilised societies were unable to accept communication of this type. Remember Joan of Arc? She was burnt at the stake for daring to suggest that she was in communion with, and guided by, the voices of St Michael and St Catherine.

She may well have been, but there is never the proof that many intellectuals hope for when dealing with this realm. Unfortunately there's also a difference in our perception of time and space as compared to that experienced in the non-physical worlds. So many people are disappointed when even the best of channels are not accurate all of the time, especially when giving information about the future. Messages are also easily misinterpreted and often misunderstood. Sometimes the words can be referring to symbolic happenings and yet they are accepted as physical fact. For example, the tidal wave that has been prophesied for so many years: some people see it as purely physical, and yet others see it as a wave of emotions that will sweep through society. Physically it is predicted to destroy many tall structures: this has also been interpreted as mankind's egos collapsing, and the start of a spiritual as opposed to a physical cleansing.

Whatever it really means, the important thing for us as individuals is to feel what is right for us, to trust in ourselves and our divinity within, and aim towards that oneness with all wisdom — our union with God — rather than relying on others to do the work for us and then complaining about the consequences.

Chapter Two

Channelled Guidance and Information

There is much talk these days about following one's guidance, and doing what feels right at a gut level rather than doing what may be logical or even expected by one's peers. But what is this guidance all about? Is it a New Age ploy to give up responsibility for ourselves, an excuse to lean on others — perhaps gurus or masters — so we can blame them for our failures and our problems? Or is it something that we can genuinely use creatively and constructively to help us live productive and responsible lives?

I believe in the latter explanation, although the former does take place all too often. People get hooked into their so-called guidance and frequently it comes from an ego wanting acknowledgement or a low-level entity. The people concerned totally absolve themselves from any responsibility for what they do or say, and follow blindly, regardless of the consequences.

I'll give you an example: a schoolteacher I used to know was becoming a slave to his inner guidance. One night he was instructed to get out of bed at midnight, and go and sit outside during a blizzard. No reason, just to do it. The next day, he was further instructed to travel the length of New South Wales. This he dutifully did, but when he arrived at the designated place, he was told to turn around and go straight home.

I asked him what all of this had accomplished other than to use up his ready cash on petrol and bring him close to exhaustion, and he answered 'obedience'. Feeling somewhat sceptical, I suggested there may have been more constructive ways to prove his obedience, and asked him what he would have done had the instructions been to jump off a cliff. A rather sheepish grin came over his face and he answered, 'I would have considered it!'. Later we checked out what had been going on, and in fact it was a lower entity masquerading as a guide.

What is important to understand is that guidance is just that — guidance. It is a form of advice or instruction that comes from within, although very often it seems to have an external source. Although this sounds like a paradox, let me explain: guidance can come from many different sources. There are many people who believe their guidance comes direct from God and see it as a source that is both within and outside their own being, as if God were both separate from and a part of their wholeness. It is similar for those who feel their information comes from the Higher Self. Most believe this is a part of the person concerned, and yet is can be talked to and also 'seen', as described by Shirley MacLaine in her book, *Dancing in the Light.*

In workshops I often give people a guided meditation specifically for them to visit their higher selves. Sometimes this takes the form of a 'wise person', and sometimes it is an image of themselves in a mirror. This image is often seen as a perfect version of themselves, the part that is clear, unemotional and totally loving. From this part comes a wisdom and clarity that can help the person on a very deep level to live his/her life in a more rewarding and fulfilling way.

In Transpersonal Psychology, the Higher Self (or Transpersonal Self as it is commonly referred to) is seen as a timeless essence, a living entity which is perceived as unchangeable, silent, a pure being. According to Piero Ferrucci in *What We May Be*, this Transpersonal Self is at the core of the superconscious, just as the personal self, or 'I', is at the core of the ordinary personality. To those who have experienced it, the realm of the superconscious and the Transpersonal Self is intensely real. It is not an intellectual concept, a by-product of the ego, or a result of suggestion. Ferrucci says: 'In its ordinary state, the personality rightly feels itself to be incomplete. Indeed, it is constantly occupied with trying to reach a state of completeness. Its usual condition is a state of perpetual "busy-ness". But the Self is in a state of plenitude and does not need to look outside in order to be fulfilled. The Self is pure BEING, beyond thoughts, beyond words, beyond actions'.

The so-called 'home' for the Transpersonal Self or Higher Self is said to be the transpersonal point that is an energy centre situated approximately 30–60 centimetres above the crown. It is also said to house 'guides' — a group of souls said to be with each person from birth until death, and another source of inner guidance (depending on your viewpoint).

Perhaps the most important point to remember about guidance is that it is within us all, and available to us all if we do but choose to tune in to it. According to Dawn Hill in her book *Edge of Reality*, 'True spiritual guidance arises from within and comes through your own mind, whether you consciously realise this or not. In order to hear the voice of guidance clearly, it is necessary that your own thoughts should be peaceful and still. Spiritual guidance, by its very nature, comes from the realms where thought is the only reality, therefore the logical place to start seeking it is within our own thought pattern': She goes on to say that spiritual guidance is very subtle:

> It operates beneath the surface and comes to you in the form of feelings, mental impressions, pictures in your mind, even in emotional spaces . . . Learning to distinguish the true guidance from false impressions is partly a matter of attitude, and partly a matter of experience. Once you have learned to recognise the Voice, you will notice that it has a unique pattern of resonance, a quality of resonance that strikes a chord of truth inside you. If you practise enough, you will eventually be able to hear it speaking in your mind.

I must also add that some people don't actually hear per se, rather they might feel, have a strong 'gut' knowing, or even receive impressions visually.

Just as we receive these impressions in different ways, so too do we differ in our beliefs as to where they come from. From my point of view, it makes no difference as to where the guidance actually comes from, provided it is of the essence — provided it is real and true. The crux is not where it comes from, but how to tell if it really is genuine. How can we know for sure that it really is the 'still, small voice within' or just our intellect feeding us new thoughts and ideas? How can we distinguish between our true inner wisdom and our ever present egos; between a higher level spiritual being and a lower level entity?

Ken Carey, author of *The Starseed Transmissions*, shared a story that illustrates so well the difficulties tied up with inner guidance, a story about himself and his wife and hearing his still, small voice. Late one night he felt he was told to go and lie down in the middle of the garden and stay there until the sun came up the next day. His ego was outraged. 'You've got to be kidding!' it said, so then there was an internal dialogue between his ego and his spirit who responded by saying, 'Trust me'. The argument continued throughout much of the night, intensified when the mosquitos started to bite (his spirit took care of that), and then it started to rain. He and his wife both got covered in mud and again the ego complained. This time the spirit promised they wouldn't catch pneumonia!

Then they started experiencing something on an archetypal level. Not only the ego left, but all the little anxieties and things that hang out on the periphery of consciousness. Carey and his wife both remembered things stretching way back, before their births, and into other lifetimes. 'We attuned to some basic, primal patterns that are being balanced on the earth through humankind, and found that we were experiencing something more important than simply what our bodies were feeling.' Come morning, they discovered they'd been out in the garden for 7 to 8 hours, and a full 2 inches of rain had fallen, yet neither of them was bitten by mosquitos and neither became sick.

This story was related in a talk given by Ken Carey. It shows that when we truly hear that voice of spirit, it tells us our most creative course, one that will lead us to the next step which will allow our body, mind and heart to bring through the next level of unfoldment. Often it doesn't take the form we expect or want, and so we turn it off or don't listen, and then complain when things don't go right.

The real difficulty here is distinguishing between the voice of our Higher Self or spirit, as Ken Carey calls it, and our egos. Our intellect constantly tries to sabotage us. Carey goes by how it feels:

If I feel attuned to my being, and calm and centred, then I can sense it. There is a quality to it that we know when we experience it. Spirit always creates harmony ... A problem is however, that often it is a *still, small* voice, and all other rambling thoughts and ideas that are passing through the consciousness may well submerge it with their volume. To me, the only answer to this is patience and trust. With experience it becomes easier to distinguish the genuine voice/feeling from the dross of everyday living and the intellect. As one tunes in regularly to the Higher Self, the time comes — sometimes sooner, sometimes later — when there is no longer any doubt. When we know without any doubt that nothing is impossible, and we have truly contacted the silence within.

Although much of this inner guidance may well be from the Higher Self, many people are aware of their guidance coming direct from God, the God Source, the God Energy. Probably the best known person to channel words of wisdom and guidance from God direct is Eileen Caddy, co-founder of the Findhorn Foundation, the spiritual community in the north of Scotland. Started in 1962, the community has grown over the years to become a Centre of Light for all to come and learn to touch into their own God within, and to live in harmony and love in a very practical and down-to-earth way. This is exemplified by the words Eileen Caddy channelled from her God source: 'Do not waste time looking at the chaos and confusion in the world, but start putting it right within yourselves'.

Eileen Caddy had meditated and studied and lived through many exceedingly difficult times. It wasn't until she was sitting in the sanctuary of Glastonbury, the ancient spiritual centre in England, that she first heard what she calls 'the voice of God'. In the stillness surrounding her, and the deep peace within her, came words in a clear, calm, yet authoritative voice: 'Be still and know that I am God'. She sat on and listened. Again the Voice came, assuring her that if she would always hear His words and follow step-by-step the guidance He gave, all would be well for her.

From that point on, Eileen Caddy has listened to the Voice and kept to the path it has shown. It has not always been easy, and certainly didn't automatically give her a life of tranquility and ease. Now, after many years, there is fulfillment and a deep inner peace, but it has taken much struggling and many heartaches to reach where she is today. Yet, looking back, she can now understand why she had to suffer so much, and how, by putting God first in all things, she gained the strength and direction to do what had to be done. 'Every experience in life, no matter how painful, which draws you ever nearer to Me, and enables you to realise that you can do nothing without Me, that you need Me at all times and in all places, is something to be everlastingly grateful for and should be accepted with deep gratitude.'

Although there were times when she lost the Voice, times when it was confused among many other voices, always, when she most desperately needed it, it would again be there in the inner silence, calm and clear. She stresses that anyone can receive clear guidance if he/she will learn to be still, and to listen and obey. 'Everyone may not hear that still, small voice as clearly as I do, but why not try to see what happens when you learn to be still and listen? Maybe you will hear something, maybe you will be aware of some action to be taken, maybe intuitively you will know what to do. Unless you try it you will never know whether it works or not. Be patient, persist, persevere, and I know you will be rewarded. Then try to live by it.'

In Chapter One I talked about the qualities that make a clear channel. Eileen Caddy is probably one of the best examples of someone who has worked hard on her own life to clear out the dross in order to channel the wisdom of God's love. She does it with simplicity and dedication, and her own life now is a spiritual example to all; yet she still keeps her feet firmly planted on the ground, very much present in the physical as well as the spiritual.

Many years ago when I was going though an extremely low or bad patch in my life, I too found the Voice at the times when I most needed it. For days it would be the one aspect of living that kept me going and enabled me to try to look positively at what was happening: 'Listen to me and I will give you comfort. Know that when you hear me, so do you feel me and know me. Know also that I am within you and yet without. You need no other to make you whole; to maintain that precious balance that is so fulfilling . . . how much more fulfilling to be the balance within yourself. I cannot promise you a life of ease, but I can promise you my love and strength, and an inner joy which will glow in your heart'.

To this day I can't say categorically whether I'm listening to the voice of God or the voice of my Higher Self, and to be totally honest, the name itself is not what really matters. It's the essence of the contact, the essence of the guidance that is important. After all, as Shakespeare wrote, 'A rose by any other name would smell as sweet'. However many people do get hooked into playing the game of 'My guidance is better than yours' or 'comes from a higher source', or whatever their ego is in need of at the time.

In fact competition is even present sometimes when people are channelling so-called guides. Whether the guidance is for themselves alone or for a wider purpose, I mistrust anyone who blatantly says that their particular entity comes from the highest level of all, and everyone must listen. However, I mistrust even more the entities who say that. I believe then it's a case of their egos still working. So many people believe that because a spirit is communicating from another dimension, he/she must be highly evolved, but this is not necessarily so. It's ridiculous to think that just because Joe Blow died yesterday and no longer has a physical body that he is now enlightened purely because he happens to be in the spirit world. Nothing could be further from the truth.

A point I need to make here is that rarely do guides or spirits actually state that they are from a high level. One knows, one feels, one senses, but it's unusual for them actually to verbalise that they're from a particular level unless they still have traces of the (physical) ego left. In fact one of the best known spirit guides of all times — Silver Birch — who spoke through British journalist, Maurice Barbanell, would not even reveal his 'real' identity. 'One day I will tell you who I am' he told the Hannen Swaffer circle where he made his presence felt as a spirit teacher of great eloquence; 'I had to come in the form of a humble Indian to win your love and devotion, not by the use of any high sounding name, but to prove myself by the truth of what I taught. That is the law'.

So what really are these guides that so many people talk about? According to Francisco Coll, the American originator of the worldwide networks Inner Peace Movement and Astra Soul (where people are taught how to communicate with their guides and use them in their daily life), these guides are spiritual helpers. As a young boy, Coll was aware of this inner guidance, and aware that he could enter into direct communciation with the source of this guidance. He teaches that before you incarnate into a physical body, you select a team of Higher Souls to help you in your life purpose. In his book *True Feelings* he states that 'They come to work with you, not for you. Your helpers give you clues for your direction... A high soul never interferes with your free will'.

One of the commonest names for these guides is 'guardian angels', as in the religious sense. Often this is more acceptable to people than trying to grasp the idea of spirit helpers constantly being around. Guides can appear in many different forms: sometimes they can be seen/felt as pure energy or light or even colour, and sometimes they seem to take on physical character- istics such as Chinese masters, Indian gurus, American Indians and so on. Some people see their guides as familiar beings who represent the epitome of love and wisdom, such as Christ or Buddha, while others don't actually see, but rather may feel, their presence. Some people can hear their guides very clearly in their minds, but are never able to visualise them, while others may perceive them as a gut knowing, or sense an opening of their own heart.

Guides don't have a sex per se — energy of itself has no polarity — however they may appear as either male or female. This is often due to their choosing an identity which we, as humans, can relate to, but sometimes it can be born of a need for the person in the physical body to achieve a specific objective. For example, a guide may come through as a feminine, healing nun so that the person can learn the qualities of softness, love and compassion. Different guides have different qualities and abilities, as do human beings. Some guides may channel material of a scientific nature; others may channel information of a more esoteric nature. Some guides are there solely for the purpose of healing, while others are with a person to help in everyday life.

Many people tune in to their guides on a daily basis. It's as simple as meditation, and the same guidelines (no pun intended) apply: to be still, to be open and receptive, and to ask for what you want. Some people are aware of a guiding force throughout their life, although they can't actually put a name to it; others are aware that guides exist, but have never heard them or been able to recognise them as such. Those who are aware of their guides use them for everything from help with making important decisions in their lives, to which route to drive the car home. They can be a really positive influence on living life constructively and with a spiritual outlook; however there are some people who abuse the role of guides and use them to make every decision, including petty ones such as what to wear, what to eat, almost to the extent of what to think, and totally give up any responsibility for their own lives.

Those people working in the field of spiritual healing often feel that their healing is channelled through a spirit guide. There is usually a very close contact with the spirit companion. Sometimes they are aware of having been together in a previous life, and the spirit has chosen to be of service — perhaps in payment of a karmic debt, or purely out of love.

Grace Cooke, one of the foremost British Sensitives of her time, was well known for her channelling of the spiritual teacher, White Eagle, founder of the spiritual centre in the UK known as White Eagle Lodge. In her book *The New Mediumship* she relates a story about her stepmother's spirit guide that seemed to offer some degree of proof in a field that has baffled scientists and researchers for years. Whilst in a trance with the Indian guide, her stepmother 'would pick up red hot coals from the burning fire, hold them, and try to pass them on to us to hold . . . when my stepmother came out of the trance, she would find her hands blackened by the burning coals, but the skin and flesh were quite normal and unburnt'.

Was it just mind control, as is possible with fire walking, or was it due to a being from another level of reality with certain ability to control fire? Apparently her guide gave another demonstration in order to prove the latter — he suspended the burning away of coal. Everyone in Grace Cooke's home went out for the day. On their return nine or ten hours later, the fire was exactly as it had been when they had left, even down to a piece of paper that had been thrown on at the last minute. The curled and blackened paper was still lying there in the same position, while the coal did not appear to have burned away at all!

It is sometimes suggested that guides are not external beings, but a secondary personality or creation of the subconscious mind of the person concerned, and in fact this may well be the case on certain occasions. According to White Eagle: 'There are cases where the medium creates a thought form and that thought form becomes animated... it becomes real enough to be seen and described, especially by novice clairvoyants who have not learnt to differentiate between a thought form and a living spirit'.

Another possible explanation for a spirit guide is that it is an extension of the person's own soul life. In other words, you may be picking up the energy of a past incarnation overshadowing you, and decide that that is a guide, for very often guides are seen as beings from a different time and different country. However, although this is a distinct possibility, it isn't always the case, and a good medium should be able to tell the difference, to feel the truth.

Sir Arthur Conan Doyle, the famous writer and spiritualist, in his book *The Return of Arthur Conan Doyle*, asks 'Does it matter greatly whether the voice that is speaking is a separate entity? What matters is whether that voice is giving you something that is pure and elevating, if it is helping you to rise above the darkness of earth. Even if it does come from your own Higher Self, does it matter?... Whatsoever is good and true and beautiful, accept and ponder in your heart'.

This brings us on to the real purpose of contact with one's inner guidance. As mentioned earlier, very often it is purely for the person doing the channelling; this was the case during the years that I daily wrote up the information I received which helped me to live my life. I know many others who have done the same — writing daily — and still continue to do just that. The information is often highly personal, usually filled with wisdom and love, and serves a very real purpose in the person's life. It offers guidance in the most positive way, but without any axe to grind. With this sort of guidance, the information comes into the consciousness and is then translated onto paper.

However, this guided writing can be taken a step further, and used to help others in their lives, such as when the information is disseminated in such a way that it can be read or heard throughout the world. According to White Eagle, although this type of writing may originate from the subconscious of the person concerned, it is very often the channelling of pure thoughts through the person's own Higher Self, and in this way can be of help and inspiration to many. For example, many of Eileen Caddy's channellings from God may be seen in this context:

Let the power of Spirit flow in and through you.
Open yourselves to this infinite power . . .

It is always there to be drawn upon
By all who are ready and prepared to use it right
For the benefit of the whole.

Another type of guidance connected with the written word is automatic writing. This involves the hand of the person being controlled by an external influence. Some people find their hands actually move over the page without any conscious effort of will; others find that their hands move over a typewriter in the same way. I used to know a lady whose hand would move so fast that the writing became totally illegible after a while, and if she didn't have a writing implement in her hand it would still move anyway, over her thigh, the table or wherever the hand happened to be — not very constructive, but it alerted her to the fact that she needed to write. What came through was usually very relevant to her life, but the writing itself was totally different from her normal everyday writing.

One of the best known authors of books transmitted through automatic writing is Ruth Montgomery. A hard-bitten American journalist and a syndicated Washington columnist on politics and world affairs, she travelled extensively throughout the USA and the world in pursuit of hard facts that would make tomorrow's headlines — an unlikely candidate for automatic writing! In her book *A Search for Truth* she tells how she first started using this method of channelled writing, and how in the early stages she was a real sceptic. It took practice and determination to overcome her scepticism. Today she stresses the importance of meditation before trying to channel, and how necessary it is to be in a state of spiritual attunement, protected by a circle of light, before commencing writing.

She uses her skills to write books on many subjects associated with psychic phenomena, spirituality, life after death and so on. Most of the information that came through her (and was subsequently printed) was information of which she had little or no knowledge before it was channelled. Nevertheless, today she is hailed as 'one of the most recognised authorities on psychic phenomena, and the most prolific representative of the spirit world'.

The author Ken Carey relates how his book *The Starseed Transmissions* was channelled and recorded over a period of eleven days during the winter of 1978–79. He then realised that his own life had been so changed by this information that he decided to share the whole transmissions.

The difficulty for some in reading this particular book is that the purported origin of the material is extra-terrestrial. However, Carey hopes that people read the book for what it contains, not for where it comes from. The messages first came to him in non-verbal form, or waves or pulsations that carried the concise symbolic content of what he calls 'meta-conceptual information'. He goes on to say that the communications presented were transmitted neurobiologically. He felt a communion with these spatial intelligences, and 'our bio-gravitational fields seemed to merge, our awareness blend, and my nervous system seemed to become available to them as a channel for communication . . . Their purpose in sending these messages has not been to teach us of themselves, but to teach us of our own nature and purpose upon this third planet from the star we call sun'. Regarding channelling itself, I will quote you some of the transmissions:

There is only one spirit, but no limit to the number of forms which this spirit can express. For the moment these forms seem important, and they are insofar as their contribution to the whole is concerned, but as the years go by, the range of the differentiation will become of much less consequence to individuals who are sincerely offering their lives as channels through which the spirit can work. As Life is able to express through such individuals with increasing ease, they will begin to recognise each other as differentiation of the same Spirit. Such individuals could be compared to conscious nerve endings, nerve endings of God in Matter, channelling the Life-flow of Christ awareness into each and every cell of the Planetary Being.

One of the most amazing channels of this century was Edgar Cayce, sometimes known as the sleeping prophet. A photographer by trade, he discovered an uncanny ability to diagnose illness and prescribe accurate treatment whilst in a deep trance state, even though he might be thousands of miles away from the person in need. He practised for 43 years, leaving behind 30,000 stenographic reports of these diagnoses when he died. These reports are now held by the Association for Research and Enlightenment at Virginia Beach, USA, along with hundreds of complete case reports containing affidavits by patients and reports by physicians.

Edgar Cayce only ever used his ability to help the sick, or to give spiritual and vocational guidance when specifically requested through what were termed 'life readings', charging little or nothing to do so. It is thought that while in his sleep-like state, Cayce was in total contact with the universal mind. One day he was asked during a reading to give the source of his knowledge, and this is what was recorded: 'It [Cayce's subconscious mind] has the power to interpret what it acquires from the subconscious mind of other individuals . . . The subconscious forgets nothing. The conscious mind receives the impression from without and transfers all thought to the subconscious, where it remains'. He said further that his 'subconscious mind was in direct communication with all other subconscious minds' and hence he was able to collect information and knowledge possessed by millions of other subconscious minds.

Once Cayce started tuning in to peoples' past lives, and explaining how or why various states had come about, the theory was put forward that the subconscious stores ALL experiences from past lives as well as from the present one. It was said that Cayce had probably learned the wisdom in one or more of his pasts, and that he was now allowing it to come through him in order to help people in the present.

The variety of his recommended treatments was considerable, and stretched from osteopathic manipulations to hot and cold packs, to specific foods, compounds, electrical treatments, massage and much more. Over the years it became apparent that if his treatment was followed to the letter, then invariably the patient would improve, often to the total amazement of the doctors in charge of the case.

Very different from Cayce, but also a person who channels information which can potentially help many people, is Ian White, a homeopath and naturopath living in Sydney. Highly regarded as a natural health practitioner, Ian White developed the 'Australian Bush Flower Essences' as a result of channelling. Similar to Edward Bach's Flower Remedies, these essences are used to bring balance when negative emotional states are prevalent in a patient. In common with many healers, he believes that good health is the result of emotional, spiritual and mental harmony, and that when patients' emotional and psychological imbalances are treated, then their diseases are cured.

Although Ian White initially used the Bach Remedies in his practice, he felt that it would be far more logical to have Australian plants healing Australians. As Edward Bach let his 'divinity within' guide him, so too did Ian White and his wife Kristin. Things started happening in a weekly meditation group: whilst in deep meditation he would be shown a particular flower, he would be told its name if he didn't already know it, and would be told of its healing properties and where he would find it growing. Sometimes he would be working with a patient on a particular issue and a certain flower would keep coming into his mind: the channelling would then follow. So began a process of collecting the various native bush flowers, from which he would then make the essences for his own practice.

Sometimes Ian experienced a particular emotional state himself when he was searching for a certain flower: when filled with obsessive thoughts out in the bush, he felt himself drawn to Boronia, and as he moved closer to the plant he started to feel better. When he found Bush Gardenia, Ian and Kristin were going through a difficult time in their relationship: this essence is now used for re-aligning people involved in a relationship. Bush Fuchsia is for integrating the left and right hemispheres of the brain: both Ian and Kristin channelled this remedy at the same time, with Ian channelling the negative conditions and Kristin channelling the positive ones. They complemented each other perfectly.

So far Ian has identified over 40 essences for use — ultimately there will be 50 — and these cover a broad range of emotional states. According to Ian: 'Their subtle action aligns the personality with the Higher Self and when this happens, true healing occurs for both the individual and the planet. The effect of the essences is similar to that in meditation: the patient accesses the wisdom of his or her Higher Self and this can help the person to resolve negative beliefs which in turn allows the healing to take place'.

These Australian Bush Flower Essences have different functions from the Bach Flower Remedies. They seem to be more suited for current issues than the Bach Remedies: Bush Iris is connected with awakening spirituality, assisting the transition process, and clearing the blocks in the base *chakra* and trust centre; Fringed Violet helps when there has been damage to the aura, or where there has been intense physical trauma such as sexual abuse or assault; Grey Spider Flower deals with extreme terror, especially the terror experienced in life-threatening situations or psychic attack.

These flower essences seem to address the issues of our time, dealing with modern man and woman in the context of life in the 'eighties and leading us into the 'nineties: Wedding Bush is used with people who have difficulty in committing themselves to relationships, and Wistaria is used for people who are uncomfortable with their sexuality. Today Ian White is still receiving information about new essences to be made, and the number of these essences on the market is increasing all the time, with more and more people benefiting from the results of this channelling.

On a different note, and affecting huge numbers of people, is Ramtha — a so-called 35,000-year-old warrior who reports that 'I am the enlightened one' and that he once lived on Atlantis. Ramtha is probably the best known of all the entities on the world scene at present, and he is channelled by J.Z. Knight, an attractive ex-housewife from Washington who has made both her name and fortune from the channellings. She has channelled for thousands across the States, and now, as videos gain wider popularity, across the world. People flock to seminars to hear Ramtha speak his words of wisdom and answer their questions in his own, unique way: 'What I am here to do is not to change peoples' minds, only to engage them and allow the wonderments for those that desire them to come to pass'.

At a huge 'Channelling Intensive' in Sydney, Australia, in November 1987, there were over 500 people crowded into the room to 'see' this very masculine presence come through — live — this very feminine lady/channel. As one onlooker put it: 'People are fascinated with the notion of an unseen personality speaking through and activating the body of another person'. Another onlooker stated: 'To be present when an entity such as Ramtha "comes" through is to find oneself with all one's doubts dispelled in a sudden and electrifying experience'.

An opposite point of view was held by a Sydney designer and artist who found that Ramtha left her with feelings of panic, fear and anger. This was to do with some of the predictions he made about natural disasters and cataclysms taking place in the near future. However, rather than taking everything Ramtha said for gospel, as many are wont to do, she was fairly objective about it all: 'I believe it could also not happen, even though Ramtha has said it will. Even a channelled entity could be wrong. Or just misunderstood. A prophet's job is to be wrong, that's why we have prophets. A prophet is only of value in telling people what could happen unless they change their ways. If what a prophet prophesies doesn't happen, he has actually fulfilled his mission'.

Another New Age spiritual entity, this time of unknown origin, is Lazaris, who speaks through Jach Pursel, a former insurance agent and now an art dealer living in Los Angeles. He is very much in demand by the rich and famous, and gives seminars from coast to coast across the USA. These seminars are noted for their simplicity, and Lazaris shuns the 'guru' tag: 'We are here to help', he says, 'and if the words that are imparted are true for you, and prove of any assistance in helping you on your search for personal and spiritual growth, then that is all that matters'.

A question that Lazaris was asked by Australia's *Unicorn* magazine is one that many are currently asking: 'Why are you and so many other entities appearing at this time?'. This is how he answered:

> The reasons are numerous. First because you have invited us. What we mean is that you as a consciousness individually and indeed collectively as a humanity, nationally and internationally, have basically said — 'We are ready to grow. We are ready to reach and stretch. We want to understand ourselves and our reality more completely and more fully, and we welcome, indeed we invite, the opportunity to learn, the opportunity to stretch, the opportunity to become more of who we are.
>
> That invitation, spoken unconsciously, subconsciously, and indeed by many very consciously, is the invitation that at this time has been put forth. Many are now coming forth to indeed impart, to give knowledge, to help you understand you and your world more completely . . .
>
> What happens among what are called the superpowers affects you on a regular and daily basis. The problems have gotten to a point where there seems to be no more solutions. Therefore in that sense, we and others are here not to give you solutions on a silver platter, clearly not, but to teach you. To teach you how to find these solutions, to teach you the changes that you need to make in your own consciousness in order to allow new solutions to become evident.
>
> We are here because you are seeking answers spiritually that your traditional methods of spirituality no longer can supply. Now it is time to expand your awareness, to expand your consciousness, to expand the horizons of your understanding. To do that you seek spiritual answers, you seek a deeper sense of your own spirituality. We and others are responding in order to offer that opportunity for you to complete your own growth.

Lazaris' ideas are very different from Ramtha's. Whereas

Ramtha talks of unavoidable doom and gloom, death and destruction, Lazaris suggests that this can be self-inflicted:

> If you indeed are bound and determined to have a year filled with doom and gloom, you can probably generate it . . . It is a time for people to look compassionately at each other, and realise there will be those who will be frightened, and those who will need help, and those who will need a loving hand, a loving touch. It is time to indeed start reaching out to each other to see what you can develop — not only within — but between . . . it is time now to start taking the energy that each has developed within — that natural resource that each person is — and start sharing it with each other, so as to see what you can create between you and the other people of your life, personally and more nationally and indeed more globally.

Although Ramtha and Lazaris have been the 'authors' of books, their main task is channelling for the masses or the individual, in person. However, there are quite a variety of books on the shelves of New Age bookstores which have been channelled directly from the universal consciousness for the purpose of transmitting wisdom and knowledge for mankind to use as it will.

Today, there are people all over the world who are in touch with this universal consciousness. Many have spent years of self-development in learning how to tap in to this wisdom and knowledge; for some it has been a swift process. Some individuals believe that they have incarnated at this time specifically to act as channels for the release and dissemination of this information, and many are strongly aware of the guiding force from within their being.

Like attracts like, and these channels seem to draw to them people of similar natures — people who intuitively feel the truth of the messages coming through, and so they form groups and/or communities to put into practice the wisdom and lifestyle advocated, that which is totally reflecting the universal consciousness. Although the inspiration received may seem different in each instant, and often reflects the personality of the group, the fundamental message is the same.

Inevitably the personality and soul consciousness of the channel is somehow, even if only slightly, imprinted on the information from the universal consciousness through the mind of the channel. Hence what comes through can be clouded or slightly coloured by the channel's beliefs and experience.

Words similar to this are written in the introduction to *The Revelation of Ramala*, a book based on channellings that took place during regular group meetings where a married couple acted as the channel. The name Ramala is taken from their soul names. Although there is much in the book that personally I don't agree with, there are also passages that make a lot of sense. One such passage, although transmitted years before the coming of Ramtha, deals with prophecy, and it's interesting to note that here doom and gloom are not predicted as definite, but are influenced by man himself:

> The true prophet, as he prophesies, recognises that the element of choice is still present, and that if Mankind itself will change, then Mankind can change what is to come . . . changes for this earth which will bring about a transformation not only of the surface of the earth, but also of life on it. This can be prophesied with certainty, but man himself, being the unknown factor on the earth, can influence the nature of this change. If only man will live in harmony, if he will only learn to sacrifice, to put others before himself, then this great transformation of the earth as it moves from one era to another, can be accomplished with a minimum of destruction, not only for Mankind on the earth, but for the earth itself.

Another book that many people feel has made a huge and valuable contribution to our times, is *The Course in Miracles*, channelled by Dr Helen Schucman. A professor of medical psychology at Columbia University's School of Physicians and Surgeons in New York, Dr Schucman was a self-proclaimed militant atheist. Having no belief in God, she resented the material she was taking down, and actually wanted to attack it and prove it wrong.

However, she spent seven years hearing the course as a kind of 'inner dictaton', and as she spent considerable time taking it down, she eventually took it quite seriously. How it all started was like this: 'The head of my department unexpectedly announced that he was tired of the angry and aggressive feelings our attitudes reflected, and concluded that there must be another way. As if on cue I agreed to help him find it. Apparently this course is the other way'.

Eventully Dr Schucman came to refer to the *Course in Miracles* as her life's work, although she remained unconvinced about its authenticity: 'I was in the impossible position of not believing in my own life's work'. Her ambivalence continued, and yet it never seriously entered her head to stop because she felt it was a 'special assignment I had somehow, somewhere agreed to complete'. When asked about the nature of the inner voice, she says: 'I do not understand the process, and I certainly do not understand the authorship. It would be pointless for me to attempt an explanation'. I've heard some people say it comes from the Holy Spirit, some that it's from Jesus Christ, and yet what is really important is not where it comes from, but whether the essence of it resonates for you as an individual.

The book is billed as a 'comprehensive spiritual teaching, a thorough and radical guide to a re-evaluation of ourselves and the world'. It has variously been described as a restatement of the New Testament, a twentieth-century book of revelation, and a modern version of Gnostic Christianity. The course tells us that at a fundamental level we are all one; that we have never really been separated from each other or from our source. In each human being there is an inherent but obscured capacity for compassion, forgiveness and peace, and it is this capacity that the course aims to awaken fully. According to the 'blurb', what stands in the way of this awakening is the ego; the course teaches how to distinguish between the voice of the ego (fear) and the voice of inner wisdom (love), thereby removing the feelings of separation that we experience, enabling us to realise our oneness with each other.

According to the course, there are only two emotions — love and fear. While we are driven by fear, we feel aggression, resentment, separation. When our inner experience is love, then forgiveness and peace of mind are our natural companions. Although this is true on one level, I find that for many people it's out of touch with reality: it is almost impossible to forgive unconditionally if you've just been raped or had your child murdered, without going through the processes necessary to release the resultant emotions such as rage, terror and pain. It's an idealistic idea, and it would be great if we could all just transmute negative emotions — but for many the release *has* to come first.

I once worked with a client who had a cancerous tumour. She had spent years in search of spiritual enlightenment, and had tried many forms of healing, but she still had the cancer. It turned out that she had been sexually assaulted as a teenager, but she was firmly convinced that she had risen above all of that, it was past and she had forgiven the person concerned. In fact she was quite upset that I should even consider there might be a connection.

In the course of the session she triggered into intense rage at what had happened to her. She was able to express emotionally all the pent-up rage, terror, helplessness and pain that she had suffered throughout the traumatic incident. When she had finally completed the releasing, she was then able to look at real forgiveness, forgiveness from her heart, not her head, which was where it had come from before. After that the healing was able to take effect and from then on the tumour started to shrink.

Don't get me wrong — I'm not saying that it is impossible to transmute emotions, only that most of us haven't reached that particular level of growth where we are so in touch with our own God within that we can actually achieve the required change on a real level.

At the end of the workbook part of *The Course* it stresses that the course is a beginning, not an end, and that no more specific lessons are assigned. 'Henceforth, hear but the Voice of God . . . He will direct your mind, and when to come to Him in silence, asking for His sure direction and His certain word.'

It would somehow be wrong to write a chapter on channelled material and not mention one of the first non-physical authors of the last twenty years — Seth. As far back as 1963, Jane Roberts, a writer and psychic researcher, and her husband, Robert, made contact with an entity known as Seth. Originally neither had any psychic background, but the information coming through from this personality encouraged them to start learning, and once Jane had gone into trance for the first time, then Seth himself was the teacher of topics as diverse as the nature of physical matter, time and reality, the God concept, reincarnation, health, and much more. The original manuscript became *The Seth Material*, published in 1970.

In January of the same year, Seth came through one day and said that he would shortly be dictating a book of his own, and gave them a complete run-down of each chapter, and what it would contain. He went on to say that the title of the book would be *Seth Speaks: The Eternal Validity of the Soul*. He started dictating the book in the same month, finishing it in August the following year. It needed little editing, and was dictated in its final draft. First published in 1972, it is a thick book filled with new concepts and understanding, and has since been published throughout the world.

Some of Seth's information has been translated into workshops, seminars, and groups everywhere. It is timeless in concept, being as relevant now as when first published: 'You create the world you know. You have been given perhaps the most awesome gift of all; the ability to project your thoughts outward into physical form'. He also says: 'The gift brings a responsibility, and many of you are tempted to congratulate yourselves on the successes of your lives, and blame God, fate, and society for your failure . . . Until you realise that you are the creators, you will refuse to accept this responsibility'.

Seth also explains about the process of Jane Roberts going into trance:

. . . there is an expansion of her consciousness and a projection of energy that is directed away from three-dimensional reality.

This concentration *away* from the physical may make it appear as if her consciousness is blotted out. Instead, more is added to it. Now from my own field of reality I focus my attention toward the woman, but the words that she speaks — these words upon the pages — are not initially verbal at all.

He goes on to explain how he can focus on a variety of simultaneous events which must be levelled out into linear expression if they are to be communicated.

> In these communications therefore, Ruburt's consciousness [Ruburt is the male soul name by which Seth knew Jane Roberts] expands, and yet focuses in a different dimension between his reality and mine, a field relatively free of distraction. Here I impress certain concepts upon him, with his permission and assent. They are not the personality who holds it or passes it on.
>
> Ruburt makes his verbal knowledge available for our use, and quite automatically the two of us together cause various words that will be spoken.

This is one explanation of the process whereby the channelled entity is able to get words and thoughts through the person concerned, and may help to clarify what actually happens. People who channel have different ideas concerning the actual process involved and in fact many channels never even think about it — channelling is something that just happens. It is the truth of the channelling that is important and whether we, as human beings, are able to incorporate what we believe to be that truth into our lives in a positive and meaningful way.

Chapter Three

Spiritual Healing

Possibly the commonest form of channelling in the world today is that of spiritual healing. It takes place in many forms, in many countries, through a wide variety of healers. It is important to note here, that anyone can heal, given the factors necessary — compassion, caring and a real desire to help.

Obviously there are those people who have a natural gift, similar to those with a talent for a musical instrument or art form, but basically healing is a natural phenomenon open to all.

The best description of someone who can heal comes from the late Harry Edwards, one of the foremost healers of this century, and one who did more to bring healers respectability and acceptance throughout Great Britain and other countries than any other healer. He stated that:

> People who have a deep inner yearning to give of themselves in healing the sick, to take away pain and stress, who possess compassion and sympathy for those who are afflicted, and are willing to sacrifice their time without any pecuniary reward; people who are generous in their nature, and who render willing service for good causes, are those who possess the spiritual qualities which mark the healing gift.
>
> This healing potential, then, only needs the development of the faculty of attunement with the spirit source of healing and the opportunity to give it practical expression.

So, what is spiritual healing? Where does it come from and how does it work? The word spiritual means literally 'of or pertaining to the spirit or soul as distinguished from the physical nature'; spirit is identified in two parts, as 'the vital principle in man, animating the body or soul as separable from the body at death' and 'a divine, inspiring or animating being or

influence'. To heal means to make whole, restore to health or
effect a cure, but it is interesting that the dictionary also gives a
couple of other definitions: 'to free from anything evil or
distressing' and 'to cleanse or purify'.

What this comes down to is a means of restoring to health
through a divine/inspiring being or influence, from a source
outside physical reality as we know it. This much is common to
all healers — that the source of their healing is outside of
themselves, and that they are just a channel or transformer for
the healing energy. However, where the energy actually comes
from seems to depend on the healers' belief systems, the society
from which they come, and the religious or cultural influences
throughout their lives.

The Rev. Noel Street, in his book *Pathways to Spiritual
Healing*, talks about this type of healing coming from a divine
source. 'Personally I have never heard spiritual healing carried
out without the use of prayer... I have seen magicians heal in
Egypt, fakirs and yogis heal in India, watched the old-time faith
healing in Wales and Britain, and helped dozens of different
healers of various denominations and colours. To me, when
prayer to a source which is beyond the mind of the healer is used,
the act has become divine.'

In the Western world, some healers believe that the healing
energy we are talking about is from the Universal Energy, but
most seem to believe that it is part of the Divine Energy from the
God source; that healing is God's gift to everyone irrespective of
race or creed, and that healing is part of the divine plan to open
man's eyes to his kinship with spirit and with God. Most
religions accept the generalisation that when a super-normal
healing takes place, it results from direct action by God.
However, many healers also believe that their healing energy
comes directly through a spirit being, a non-physical entity in
the spirit world who may have been in some branch of the
medical profession when last in a physical body.

For those who have difficulty grasping this concept, have a
look at the following diagram which may help to clarify
matters. The God energy is at the top of the pyramid, and
gradually this is transformed through intermediaries directly to
those in need in our physical reality.

'But why can't God heal me direct?' you might well say. He can. However, many people, churches and religious organisations pray for healing miracles, and although they do happen, they are in the minority when compared with the regular 'supernormal' healings that take place through healers around the world. For example, Harry Edwards, in his book *The Evidence for Spiritual Healing* cites over 6000 cases taking place within a four-year period, and he was but one healer in a country which has literally thousands of healers, many of whom have as high a success rate. Despite this, there are many churches, both orthodox and non-orthodox, that hold regular healing services all the year round, and these churches are often packed with people in search of help and relief from suffering.

Some people believe that healing needs the intermediary because the energy from God might be too powerful for the physical body to handle; hence the role of the healing spirit is to transform this energy into an acceptable state.

Despite the miracles that take place, it's worth remembering that healers are also normal human beings. They live a normal physical life, and just happen to have spent time developing their abilities of attunement and compassion, as well as learning how to bypass their intellect in order to allow the healing energy to come through their being. It's the same with the spirit helpers — they are normal spirit beings. Just because they no longer have a physical body does not mean that they are perfect, or even have all the answers; in fact they are often learning as much as we are, and they can't bypass the laws of spirit any more than we can bypass the laws of man.

In the book *Healing Hands*, by J. Bernard Hutton, the author interviews Dr William Lang, an ophthalmic surgeon who died in 1937, but now works and speaks through the body of George Chapman. This is what Lang says in an interview to Hutton:

> God is what I see in everything that is good; and when I am healing I am doing the work of God. God is simply a Great Love ... we are here to do God's work...
>
> When you pass over here, you retain the same personality as you had on earth. Some people who come to see me say: 'You are such a wonderful spirit person Dr Lang' and I tell them: 'Now, look here, young lady, or young man, when I lived on earth, I liked to live my life to the full. I tried to do good and not to wilfully harm anyone, but I was NEVER the PERFECT being. And now that I have passed into the spirit world, I am still the SAME William Lang as I was upon earth. I know a little more about my work, but as for changes in myself — there are none, I am still the SAME person. You see, people believe that when you pass over here, you become very wonderful, but you do not. You remain the same...'

There has been much well-documented research to prove that this unlikely partnership between the surgeon, Dr Lang, and the ex-fireman, George Chapman, not only works, but that the spirit being working with Chapman really is Dr Lang. There are testimonies from people who knew Lang when he was in a physical body, including one from his daughter. Some of these testimonies are from people on whom Lang had worked whilst in the physical. This time round, he not only recognised them again, but mentioned incidents that only the real Dr Lang could have known.

So, back to the healing process. How does it actually work? Let's look at the energy coming from the God force into a spirit/healing intelligence, and so into a healer. The healer attunes with the healing intelligence and with the patient, and the energy is transmitted through the channel, via the hands and the heart, and into the patient. The healing energy seems to augment and speed up the natural healing process/ability within the person. However, it is slightly more complex than just that.

Every change in the universe is the result of law-governed forces, and our bodies are subject to definite laws which control our health from birth until death. Spiritual healing, according to Harry Edwards, is the result of law-governed healing forces that induce change. For any state of change to be purposefully affected, intelligent direction is needed to administer the law-governed forces to the subject. It therefore stands to reason that effective administering of a healing force requires intelligent direction — that which originates from the spirit realm. Edwards writes: 'When spiritual healing succeeds with an "incurable" condition, it denotes that a wiser intelligence than that of man is responsible for the law-governed, ordered change. If this intelligence is not earthly, then it must be of spirit'.

In a successful healing, the directing intelligence is able to administer the remedial force/energy to induce a state of beneficial change within the patient. In fact, the healing forces are able to create a chemical change, when necessary, through the application of one given form of energy to another. What is especially interesting is that a) the effects of these healing forces influence only diseased cells or structure — they never disturb healthy ones, and b) in this type of healing the healer does not need to know or even understand the full extent of the problem.

Many years ago I learnt this lesson, much to my surprise. I had been giving a friend some healing purely to induce a state of relaxation as she was under considerable nervous tension. She relaxed fairly well, and went on her way calmer and more together. I thought nothing more about it. A week later I saw her again, and she thanked me profusely for curing her long-standing gynaecological condition. I had had no knowledge that she even had a physical problem, let alone what it was, and obviously I hadn't needed to know. At one level, something beyond myself — maybe this spirit intelligence — had taken over. Since then it's happened many times, and other healers report similar occurrences.

To give you an example of how the healing energy can affect a chemical change, I'll describe an experience that took place in the UK over a decade ago. Just prior to Harry Edwards' death, I spent an afternoon at his healing sanctuary to observe his work.

He suggested I sit with him so that I could actually feel what he was doing with one of his patients. She was a middle-aged lady who had been immobilised from rheumatoid arthritis (RA) for over 20 years. Having been a physiotherapist, I had worked with many cases of RA, and had felt many rigid and calcified joints, but hers were certainly some of the most unyielding. For her to look to the side, she had to turn her whole body, because her spine was locked solid. She could bend, albeit slightly, from her hips alone.

She sat on the healing stool rather hesitantly, and briefly told Mr Edwards her story, and he suggested I examine her back. He then took one of my hands and placed it at the base of her neck, covering it with his own hand. He guided my other hand slowly over the prominences down her spine, resting briefly on each one. At each stop, I felt the joint click beneath my fingers, and in about 5 minutes, every joint in that woman's vertebral column had unlocked. She turned her head for the first time in 20 years, she moved her back, she bent to both sides, and then she burst into tears.

On questioning her later, I discovered that the doctors had done everything they could, and eventually had told her to rely on strong analgesics when she could no longer tolerate the pain which she would have to suffer for the rest of her life. Instead, she chose to try spiritual healing, and what resulted was a miracle that will stay with her for the rest of her life.

From my viewpoint, it seemed that the calcification that had been present in the joints had been impeding movement, and had become totally dispersed by a mere touch of the healer's hands. It was instantaneous, and yet sometimes such healing can take considerable time to effect a cure, and sometimes, of course, little (if anything) happens at all. Healers are only the channel for the healing energy, therefore they can no more blame themselves for failures than they can take credit for successes. What happens, and the timing involved, is not under their conscious control. All healers can do is mentally ask for the healing energy to flow through them for the highest good of all concerned.

So why is it that some people are healed and others are not? As stated before, as there are physical laws governing the material world, so too are there laws governing the spirit world, and we cannot transgress these laws. For instance, healing cannot 'grow' another limb if one has been amputated, and yet it may cure the condition that was leading to the amputation. If the cause of the disease is still present, then the healing cannot be fully effective: if arthritis stems from living in damp surround-ings and poor diet, then these conditions must be changed before a cure can be completed. Similarly, if the cause is of emotional origin, the condition cannot be altered until the actual original cause, the anger, resentment, fear or grief, is released.

I'll give you a couple of examples of the importance of removing the cause in healing. A frozen shoulder is a condition where there is often calcification within the shoulder joint, and thickening of the tendons around the structure, leading to intense pain and lack of mobility. On two separate occasions I worked with patients with frozen shoulders who both had identical symptoms, and yet the treatments were totally different.

One of them, a young woman in her early twenties, couldn't move her arm at all. She wore a sling, and the slightest movement at all triggered tears of pain. She had had the condition on and off for seven years, had tried everything, and now was desperate. All I did was to channel healing into her shoulder joint for a period of 20 minutes. At the end of that time she was completely free of pain and could move her arm with totally free-range movement. I suggested she stay off salt as I felt that that had contributed to her condition, and for a year she was clear of trouble. When it flared up the next time, she had started eating salt again!

The other frozen-shoulder patient was also a young woman, on a good diet, but in a lot of pain. It turned out that she was very unhappy in her life: a situation had arisen that had angered her considerably, but she had been unable to do anything about it. Although she hadn't realised it at the time, her shoulder had deteriorated since then. After a few minutes of healing energy, she was able to contact the pent-up rage inside her, and once she had screamed and physically beaten out her anger — as if her arm had no problem at all — she was totally without pain, and once again could move her arm normally: the emotional energy causing the problem had been released.

The healing we've just been discussing is that taking place when the healer's spirit self is in a state of attunement with the healing energy or spirit intelligence, and also with the patient's spirit self. It is a common experience, especially for healers developing the gift of healing, to consciously feel the pain of the condition within the patient as a part of this attunement. It is an impression on the healer's consciousness, and one which in time and with experience, is controllable and no longer necessary.

This type of healing takes place while the healer is totally conscious, but healing also takes place in situations where the healer/medium allows a particular healing intelligence, often a spirit doctor, to take over his/her body and voice and perform the healing directly.

According to Dr Lang (via George Chapman), 'Spirit healing is healing FROM spirit, THROUGH spirit, TO the spirit body of the patient, and thence to the physical body of the patient'. Using healing vibrations (of a divine source) direct from God, Lang takes over Chapman's body completely — Chapman has no conscious awareness afterwards — and works directly on the spirit body of the patient by drawing it slightly away from the physical body which it is normally wrapped around. This puts the spirit body in a proper condition to be attended to — in other words, the vibrations are created whereby it becomes 'alive' and those organs which were previously tiny, according to Lang, assume their right size, and he can operate.

Many people feel it hard to accept the concept of each of us having a spirit body when it is invisible to the naked eye. However, Lang describes how he can actually 'see' both the physical and spiritual bodies of a person, and he can also see the aura (an electromagnetic radiation surrounding the body) which is constantly moving and changing colour, and exists approximately 5 centimetres or 2 inches (depending on the state of health) away from the body. Each organ in the body reflects a definite colour in the aura, but when the organ is diseased, the reflection changes colour.

To remove a tumour from the physical body, Lang will

perform an invisible and painless operation on the spirit body of the patient, and by removing the tumour from this spirit body, will bring about changes in the physical body.

The other method of healing that Dr Lang employs is injecting what he describes as 'astra fluid' into the organ of the spirit body — a rather uncanny sight for the watcher. It resembles science fiction movies in which an invisible man performs extraordinary feats without a physical body, while all the implements are visible — but in reverse. This time the man is visible, but the instruments are not, and yet you see the movements as if there were physical instruments present.

An interesting aspect of George Chapman's channelling of Dr Lang is that having operated on the spirit body and closed the wounds, scars are left which sometimes remain for a brief period on the human body. However, no pain is felt, and these scars heal very rapidly. A fascinating anomaly occurs with these operations: Dr Lang operates with his left hand, making all the movements one would expect of a skilled surgeon during a physical operation. George Chapman is right-handed!

Another world-famous healer in a similar field was the Brazilian, Ze Arigo, who channelled the German Dr Fritz. Once entranced, Arigo would perform physical operations which would take place without anaesthetic, sterile techniques or even proper instruments. Arigo had only two years of schooling before he was dismissed because he was said to be too stupid to be allowed to continue. However, his life was exceptionally well documented, and this uneducated labourer made many instantaneous diagnoses using modern technical descriptions of the various problems (such as retinoblastoma as opposed to eye trouble) and invariably these diagnoses would be totally accurate.

The leader of the largest group of researchers into Arigo's healing was Andrija K. Puharich MD, a man who spent years in electronics research before turning to parapsychological research. Writing about Arigo in 1963, after the first time he had witnessed him healing, Puharich commented: 'I watched Arigo doing surgery without anaesthesia or antisepsis; every patient was helped, and none had post-operative complications. It was truly a mind-shattering experience to see every principle of surgery violated with impunity. Indeed I found myself unable to accept the data of my own senses'.

Instead of merely watching Arigo, Puharich decided to put the healer to the test of operating on him personally: he had a benign tumour on his right elbow. The Brazilian borrowed a pocket knife from one of the many people crowding into the office/surgery, and excised the lump in a matter of seconds without Puharich feeling any pain. However, the doctor still wasn't completely convinced. Knowing that Arigo's hands were dirty, and that the knife he had used was unsterilised, there was a good chance of infection setting in. When nothing happened, and the small wound healed in three days, his doubts disappeared.

Arigo's spirit control, Dr Fritz, not only 'talked' into Arigo's ear when diagnosing, but also told him what drugs a person should take at any particular time. For the operations themselves, Dr Fritz would take complete control of Arigo's body. Afterwards Arigo, like George Chapman, would have no conscious recollection of anything that had happened; in fact when he was shown a 90-minute film of himself operating on patients, he fainted!

However Dr Puharich, even after five years study of Arigo's work, was still unable to decide whether Dr Fritz really was a spirit entity or an aspect of Arigo's own personality, even though he spoke in a thick, gutteral voice, and had mannerisms totally different from Arigo's.

One country that has produced many of these psychic surgeons is the Philippines. Tony Agpaoa, one of the more reputable ones, had many cures to his credit as well as failures. A German investigator, Alfred Stelter, described an operation on an American woman who had severe breast cancer; he and his team filmed the operation using six different movie cameras. Stelter writes in his book *PSI Healing*:

> The operation took between two and three minutes during which time the patient suffered no pain, the healer used no instrument (only his fingers) and the operation left no scars. Throughout, everything was carefully watched and filmed to check that nothing external was secreted as

evidence. Physicians handled the excised tissue afterwards and concluded that it consisted of organic fleshy matter.

On returning to Germany, Stelter's films were processed. They proved that no trickery had taken place, and that the original observations in Baguio were correct.

Although Agpaoa was known to be one of the genuine healers while he was alive, there are frauds who deal in animal flesh and blood. I have come across people who returned to Australia from the Philippines claiming cures for diseases they never knew they had, having received the Holy Spirit for the sum of $150.00!

Although I do believe there are genuine healers in the Philippines, I was not very happy with what I saw there in 1984. My husband and I were there for an International Conference on Paranormal Healing, so we had access to many of the healers in Baguio, Manila and Pangasinan. One local surgeon, despite an international reputation, left me feeling most disturbed. Although he would hold a brief service in his chapel first, he performed like a factory hand, completing approximately 200 operations in 2 hours flat. There was no caring, no follow-up, and little sensitivity towards the patients, many of whom had travelled thousands of miles to be healed, and were often still in a state of shock after their 'operation'.

Back home in Australia I have watched a Philippine-trained psychic surgeon operate a few times. This man is a healer in the true sense of the word. He uses the surgery gift as an adjunct to his natural health practice, and only when guided to do so. As his hands enter the physical body, he appears to be in a totally altered state, the energy in the room heightens considerably, and stays that way until the operation is over.

I had my hands on a patient during one of these operations; the patient was German, with a very poor command of English, so there was no way it could have been a case of mind control or hypnosis as some people suggest. As a result of his condition, the man's heart rate was dangerously fast, and his blood pressure high. At the exact moment that the surgeon removed some sort of blockage from within, the heart rate magically dropped to a normal, steady pace. When the patient got off the table, he was a much healthier colour, and his energy was obviously flowing more freely.

This particular healer had in the past been sick himself, and had faced death on more than one occasion before he was given the gift of healing. He had tried both orthodox and alternative medicine before he found his 'cure', and as a result, he dedicated the remainder of his life to healing and serving others in need.

When working, he is 'tuned in' to a higher vibration, and not in trance as are some other healers. He is one with 'the still, small voice' I have mentioned before, and uses the God energy from the universe to perform the operations. He feels this is possible because he *is* in a physical body, and so can work on others also in physical bodies. If he gets an internal stop signal, then he knows it is not right to perform surgery, and he trusts that signal implicitly: the condition of the patient might be karmic, and he knows he has no right to interfere.

In his work he stresses the importance of a change of lifestyle, stress level, attitude, nutrition and bad habits, as surgery only removes the end result of a cause which, left unattended, will create new problems for the person. For this and other reasons, he uses surgery only occasionally and follows it up with wholistic health care. His patients generally leave the surgery feeling better, more relaxed and positive, and with greater understanding of their condition.

Another healer, who also works wholistically but in a different manner, and not using surgery, is South African-born Andrew Watson, now living in Australia. He has been a pioneer of energy balancing in the West, and has successfully blended Eastern philosophy and Western psychology. He has spent many years working with the energy systems, or *chakras*, of the body, and has developed a system of 'mapping' this *chakra* system which has proven effective in thousands of case studies, and applicable to people living in both Eastern and Western societies.

Like many healers, myself included, Andrew Watson believes in reaching the cause of the problem in order to effect true healing. This cause, he believes, usually stems in some way from blocked energies: any emotion that a person has experienced — at any time in their life — but has not expressed, will become locked into the body, and will remain within rigidified muscular tissue and body armour.

It is now possible to relocate these blocks using the seven major *chakras*, and to release them. To do this, it is necessary to work in a wholistic way. He sees healing as a move towards wholeness, a method of incorporating all modalities, and hence his role is to act as a catalyst for personal transformation within the person being healed. Thus he is of the firm belief that the healer is only the facilitator of what, essentially, is an internal and individual process.

Andrew Watson feels that no one method of healing is suitable for every patient; it is what is needed at a particular moment that is important. He balances a combination of magnetic-type laying on of hands with energy balancing and (psycho) therapy as appropriate. He also brings in the transpersonal perspective: this gives an overview of life which is in touch with our purpose for being here, on earth, at this time. As Jung said, 'A life without purpose is a neurotic one'. Andrew Watson feels that any one of these healing methods alone is not enough. It's the combination that acts so powerfully, with the added utilisation of the universal energy which is freely available to anyone, anywhere, at any time. It is here that the heart centre, mentioned in Chapter 1, comes into its own.

In the book *Healing Music* by Andrew Watson and Nevill Drury, Watson says: 'The heart, in healing terms, is the transformer used to convert universal energy into the healing force of unconditional love. This is a love that has no expectations and no demands, and is given freely with no thought of any return'. To me, this typifies the differences between the many types of healing appearing these days under a variety of names, and the healing we have been referring to. The former types of healing seem to bypass the heart centre, and the energy which comes through seems to be a 'colder' type of energy with no heart in it.

Returning to our discussion of healing using the practice of channelling, another method is that employed by Tom Johanson, the current secretary of the Spiritualist Association of Great Britain. With clinics throughout Europe as well as in London, this healer's particular speciality is manipulating joints through 'softening' the bones and structures surrounding a painful or damaged area. He transmits the healing energy through his hands into the locked joint (or joints), and at the particular moment when it 'softens', he manipulates it, often with miraculous results. He's had no training in osteopathy or any other field of medicine, but allows the healing energy to flow through him as necessary. It is a powerful experience, and I have watched him heal rigid backs and painful necks very simply.

Throughout this discussion of different healing methods, not much has been mentioned as to what the person receiving the healing actually feels or experiences. There can be a wide variety of feelings, although the commonest is one of warmth or even intense heat at the site of the healing. Sometimes cold may be experienced, and often there is tingling or a pins-and-needles sensation. Although both patient and healer usually experience the same temperature effect, it is also possible for one to feel warmth while the other feels cold.

Until recently, these temperature changes were totally undetectable by any known scientific methods. However, over the years, several countries have made long strides in the field of paranormal research, and now scientific instruments are available which are able to record the various temperature changes. The implications of such advances are huge, for no longer can sceptics say that this type of healing is all in the mind, and that all healers must be frauds.

Other reactions that can take place are as varied as feeling intense well-being, to feeling nauseous; feeling deep relaxation to feeling stirred up emotionally, and so on. On occasions I've also worked with clients with chronic conditions, and the healing has stirred up so much pain that they have been in tears. Such occasions are rare, fortunately, but invariably each client has reported back after a few days saying that the original condition has either lessened considerably, or completely cleared up. It's as if the healing brings the pain up to the surface in order to release it. Laughter is another reaction that can take place as a result of healing, and so too is sleep.

Channelling healing energy can also be the means by which a person can be triggered into deep-seated emotional issues. I worked with a client recently, and as part of the healing, I put one hand over her root *chakra* at the base of her spine. This is the centre to do with survival, power, aggression, and the basic fear of being here in this incarnation: within a matter of seconds, she had spontaneously triggered into the immediate moments after her birth. These moments had been so traumatic that they had contributed to the long-term problems she was currently facing. As a result of that particular session, she was able to release a huge emotional block, and her life changed considerably for the better.

So far the only type of healing we've been talking about has been contact healing. There is also another type of healing that takes place, not only in places throughout the world, but across the world. This is known as absent or distant healing. It is the term given to the treatment of a patient who is not physically in the presence of the healer at the time. The proximity of the patient to the healer is irrelevant, distance making no difference at all. It's as if the healing energy has no limitations of space and time. This has been illustrated time and again where help has been sought for others by friends or relatives, often without the knowledge of the sick person concerned, and at the time the healer attuned to the patient, he or she took a miraculous turn for the better.

One particular case clearly illustrates the validity of absent healing. Harry Edwards was interrupted in his work by a couple, from the north of England, whose son was dying of spinal meningitis in Portsmouth, in the south. They had been urgently summoned and, expecting to be too late, had broken their journey as a last hope. The healer immediately went into the 'silence' and sought help for the couple's son.

When the parents arrived at Portsmouth Hospital, they found their son sitting up in bed with four doctors in conference around him, studying what seemed nothing short of a miracle. All traces of the disease had vanished, and so remarkable was the recovery that the young man was allowed to return to full military duty, although complications are quite common following this particular disease.

Absent healing may well be one of the commonest methods of healing taking place in society today. Healers throughout the world are known to have healing lists. These are often extremely long lists of patients requiring help: sometimes the requests have come from the people themselves, at other times the requests have been made by friends or relatives. Many people who have been helped themselves by this method of healing, but know that their friends firmly believe in the abilities of the medical profession, will ask for aid without the knowledge of the person concerned, and when the miracle occurs (shattering the medical fraternity) they have a pretty clear idea of what has happened!

Many small groups sit together on a weekly basis in order to pray for healing for people they know, but there are different methods of absent healing, prayer being just one. For those working with spirit guides it seems to be simply a question of getting into a state of attunement and mentally giving the details of the person concerned, where they are, their name, and so on, and then asking the guide to go and give the healing. With this type of absent healing there is usually a proviso that the healing be for the highest good of the person concerned, so that if on some level the person doesn't want it, then it can't be forced upon them.

Another method of distant healing is for the healer to sit down and tune into the energy of the person concerned. Some healers may tune into an object belonging to the person to forge a closer connection. Either way they will then mentally image the energy flowing into the person at the relevant spot, or visualise light flowing into their whole being. With visualisation techniques it's possible for some healers to tune in to the condition itself and then send healing to the cause of the problem, or the energy centre that is affected.

I had an interesting experience recently using one of these healing methods. I received a phone call late one night from some people with whom my daughter was staying. They said that my daughter was really sick, and that they had nothing in the house to give her; they were loath to call a doctor at that late hour unless it was a dire emergency. As they were 4 hours drive away from where I was, there was nothing I could do physically, so I suggested that I send some healing. Luckily my daughter had gone into a feverish sleep by this stage, so she had no idea about our frantic phone conversation.

I went into a meditative state, very clearly visualised her body, saw the area that needed the healing, and mentally filled her with the light energy. At 8 o'clock the following morning she rang me as if nothing had ever been wrong. She had had no conscious knowledge of what had happened, but she had received the healing totally, and was completely back to normal.

Andrew Watson uses yet another method of sending absent healing. He gets the patient to acquire a growing plant, and then teaches him/her to use it as a focal point to 'keep their attention'. He then focuses energy on a plant of his own, which seems to pass this energy through the plant kingdom, across the world to the patient's plant, from which point the healing energy reaches the patient directly.

He cites a case that took place a few years ago while he was living in South Africa. A patient diagnosed as having terminal leukaemia was given two weeks to live. She was presented with a plant to focus on daily, and the healer focused daily on his. This took place twelve years ago now, and the person is alive and well, with no signs of leukaemia. The plant, apparently, is also thriving!

Sometimes, however, the plant can die, as if absorbing the sick energies has been its whole purpose of existence and when the person concerned is better this purpose has ceased. Nevertheless, in many cases the plant ends up being much loved and healthy, as in the instance described. Watson found a dramatic rise in the success rate of his absent healing once he started utilising the plant kingdom. Maybe this is a source of untapped energy we could all do well to look at...

Although over the years the channelling of healing energy has taken place throughout the world, it has always been frowned upon by the medical fraternity: in some countries medical practitioners were struck off the register if they were discovered to have co-operated with non-medical healers. However in 1977 a monumental step was taken by the General Medical Council of Great Britain. It not only accepted alternative healing practices in general, it suggested that doctors should familiarise themselves with such practices so as to be able properly to refer their patients, and be competent to judge the healer involved. In many hospitals throughout England, healers are actually allowed to work quite openly, provided it is with the knowledge and consent of the doctor in charge of the case.

It is important to note here that spiritual healing doesn't always lead to instantaneous cures. As one well-known healer in Europe once said: 'All spiritual healing is miraculous, but often a series of little miracles rather than one big one'. An important point to remember, however, is that nothing is impossible in this particular field: it is only our minds that have constraints and limitations. To quote from the Rev. Noel Street: 'The power and depth of the Silence is boundless. We are the only limitations ourselves. It is only the boundary of our mind which fences us from all-mind, our spirit from all-spirit, our love from all-love, our faith from the faith, which can move mountains, and our healing power from God's power'.

There are channels all over the world allowing this spiritual energy to flow through them as healing energy: those who regularly go into the silence within to hear the Voice; those who have listened to the words from the Bible, 'Go forth...and heal the sick'; and those whose life is dedicated to healing with love and joy.

Chapter Four

Mediumship

Mediumship is a process whereby a spirit is allowed to use the body and speaking apparatus of a person for the purpose of healing and the dissemination of information. A medium acts as a transformer for the energy of spirit to have access to this reality, a bridge between this world and the next, and so facilitate communication between those in the physical world and those who have passed on.

Deep trance mediumship occurs when the person concerned enters a sleep state in which he or she is totally oblivious to anything taking place around or through him/her. The medium may become animated, may walk around with open eyes and even talk to people, but afterwards has no conscious recollection of anything that has been said or done.

A conscious medium channels a spirit being while usually remaining aware of what is being said. The experience is similar to hearing yourself talk, but as if you are hearing the words through a fog, and has to be done without choosing or controlling the words. It is a little disconcerting to hear yourself saying words and sentences that you have no conscious knowledge of, and there is sometimes a sense of 'Am I really saying those words?' It is also hard to remember the details after the event: to me it's as if only part of my consciousness has been present, and although I might get an understanding of what has been said, the details rarely remain. The easiest way to describe it is to think of myself as withdrawing in order to allow another being to come in to my space. It's as if I move backwards and the spirit steps in front to take over the reins for the allotted time.

With conscious mediumship, it is the responsibility of the person acting as the medium to discriminate with regard to matters concerning both the entity itself and the words. He or she has to do this without actually changing what comes through, yet still ensuring that only the truth is spoken. This brings up the importance of the intention: that the spiritual energy should only come from the highest source, and that the medium should be clear and open. According to Dawn Hill, author of *Edge of Reality* and *Reaching for the Other Side*, with a trance medium it is different. Here it is the responsibility of the person acting as the control on the physical level to discriminate as to the spirit coming through. This control is concerned with maintaining the safety and well-being of the medium the whole time he or she is in the deep trance state.

Dawn Hill speaks from years of experience acting as control for her husband, Roland, who is a deep trance medium. In *Edge of Reality* she writes: '[The control] should ensure that everyone present at a trance sitting knows and understands the rules that are to be followed. When a medium enters a trance state, his rate of vibrationary frequency is altered... the heightened level of frequency affects every cell in Roland's body as well as the energies within his aura. If anyone were to touch him, even lightly, while he is in this altered state, the results would be both severe and painful, possibly even fatal'. The only exception is in a healing session — where in many cases the medium obviously comes into contact with his/her patient — in which case the spirit will adjust the frequencies so that the contact is harmless.

The trance state can best be described as a partnership between the medium and the spirit entity. Although in some cases it appears as if the spirit or entity controlling the medium is holding the medium's mind in a hypnotic state, taking possession of the whole body, in fact it is a system born out of mutual co-operation. The medium will surrender to the entity, putting her personality into abeyance while the discarnate personality takes control.

In the book *The New Mediumship* by Grace Cooke, the author's well-known spirit guide/teacher, White Eagle, says that 'This is done by the powerful projection of our thought through the chakras and therefore through the human nervous system'. However, he goes on to say that communication between the two worlds is a very delicate matter, and can easily be thrown off balance. 'The nervous system of the medium is easily impaired unless proper care is taken, which means care of the health, care of living conditions, but it also requires care of the soul and spirit of the instrument.'

Still talking about the communication between the two worlds he explains that it can sometimes be difficult to hold on to these lines of communication. '[This] is where conditions sometimes get broken, when there is disturbance or noise or a violent inharmonious mental instrusion. It requires much practice to hold the line firmly when so little can break the contact.'

I can certainly vouchsafe as to this difficulty, having watched many people trying to hold a trance in the face of every imaginable kind of interruption. However, even more important to remember is the devastation that a disturbance of this kind can cause to an unsuspecting medium. I have experienced the painful results of a cat jumping onto my lap whilst in a deep meditative/trance state, and it is similar to a profound shock to the whole nervous system. It was as if the physical presence of the cat had 'earthed' me, and somehow shattered the built-up psychic energy.

I recently did some channelling in a similar deep state, and afterwards went too quickly into a situation where there was loud, jangly music. It felt as if my whole nervous system was exploding, and the pain and internal cacophony in my head was so intense that for a few moments I felt close to insanity. I wanted to scream, and yet the scream was locked inside my head. It was a terrifying experience, and it took quite a while, and a lot of help from two healer friends, to come back to normal — not to be recommended under any circumstance!

In deep trance the medium takes on all the characteristics of the controlling entity. There is often a total change of voice, mannerisms, and phraseology, and yet outwardly nothing may appear different, although I have watched people's faces change shape, such as the eyes appearing more slanting or the nose becoming negroid-looking. The transition from being in full control to being in trance is mostly an easy one, the medium often appearing to have fallen asleep. However, sometimes it can be a struggle, such as when a spirit is speaking for the first time (they have to become used to controlling a new physical body and speaking apparatus) or when the entity is from a very high level, or even from a different planet.

I talked to one entity who complained that entering the

physical body felt like being encased in a block of concrete! He seemed to have a hard time adjusting his vibrations to this level, and then seemed to find it hard to stay in the particular body for more than a short time.

However, most partnerships between medium and spirit are born out of mutual trust and experience, and they become well used to working with each other. One of the longest standing partnerships ever was that of Maurice Barbanell and Silver Birch, the Indian spirit who was a well-known teacher/guide. For over twenty years no-one knew who actually channelled Silver Birch, although much of the information coming from him was made known to the public.

People are often concerned that information coming from a medium might be coming only from the medium's subconscious, and not from another realm at all. This certainly can and does take place, and it is as well to be aware of the possibility. However, it is usually possible to tell the difference, especially when you get used to working with people in the trance situation. But what is really important is the content of what is coming through. If that is valid, then does its source really matter?

In the book *Guidance from Silver Birch*, the editor, Anne Dooley, notes that Hannen Swaffer (the leader of the circle where Silver Birch used to appear) pointed out that in vital respects the two personalities of Barbanell and Silver Birch totally contradicted each other. One main area of contradiction was that Silver Birch taught reincarnation, while Barbanell eschewed it, yet in trance he confounded his own conscious argument!

However, Anne Dooley herself received quite a shock the first time she witnessed Barbanell in trance. 'What had happened to the caustic-tongued, cigarette-smoking wisecracking journalist to whom I was daily professionally accustomed? Freud has long familiarised us with the dynamics of the subconscious in his analyses of psychoses and the tell-tale creative activity of our dream life. ...This was another personality speaking through the body of the man I knew well in daily life. But it was not the man himself; it was NOT his style.'

Apparently one leading South African spiritualist, Edmund

Bentley, described the difference between Silver Birch and Barbanell as 'startling'. He wrote that:

> Barbanell is a competent public speaker . . . [he has] the ability to tell a witty story and, above all, to present a case in the manner of a courtroom barrister.
>
> But Silver Birch . . . brings a grandeur and authority, compound of that higher realm of simplicity and love which has the hallmark of kingship. His mighty range of description, his immaculate choice of words and his sheer silver, glowing oratory combine to prove, if any proof were needed, that here is another being, a visitor from the realms of spirit, one who has taken over the earthly vessel and filled it with an authentic cornucopia, distinct, individual and apart.

Barbanell described the evolution of his complete trance control as something that took place slowly, and it took years before he achieved complete unawareness of what was being said by Silver Birch. He explained how it also took time for Silver Birch to gain mastery over the English language, with the original gutteral accent being replaced with a pleasant but deeper sounding voice than Barbanell's own. To him, trance was a willing surrender:

> I compose myself, try to make myself passive and mentally offer myself, praying that the highest, best and purest that are possible shall come through me. Then an unusual feeling of warmth steals over me . . . Gradually I lose awareness of my surroundings and appear to be enveloped in a comforting kind of blanket, and then 'I' have gone. Where 'I' have gone to I do not know...I am told that trance is achieved by my guide blending his aura with mine, and then taking control of my subconscious mind. The awakening is a process that reverses the entry into trance...

Although it is mostly true that the process of becoming entranced is gentle and non-traumatic, I have witnessed occasions when it's been hard for either the spirit to enter the medium, or for the medium to accept the spirit. In fact on one memorable occasion it took quite some time for the entity to accustom itself to the medium's body, and when it did, it proceeded to whistle for the next 20 minutes! I have to confess that I was unable to stop myself from laughing, and to this day I have no idea who or what it was, or what it was all about. It wasn't a negative experience, just different.

According to Stewart Wavell in the book *Trances*, when a person enters a trance, the hypothalamus, a section at the base of the brain which controls our basic drives, ceases to function normally. Most (but not all) of the sense receptor cells in the hypothalamus become inactive, and so the person having the experience 'loses his senses'. Wavell adds: 'In trance, the channels of communication to the brain seem to be disconnected: information cannot get through; and the hypothalmus, the control centre, continues an existence, apparently independent of our senses'.

The question that is so often asked of trance mediums, especially since the advent of Ramtha and Lazaris has allowed channels to become more accessible to questioning, is 'What happens to the personality of the medium whilst he/she is in trance?'.

According to White Eagle (talking about Grace Cooke),

Her personality is not functioning here. Her soul is withdrawn to a higher state. Nevertheless, so close a connection exists between her and the physical condition that if anything were to happen that she did not like, she would at once return to her body. When she is in trance she is raised in consciousness, and what takes place during a trance lecture is recorded by her soul in that higher state of consciousness; but on returning to the body the memory is obliterated. Later perhaps, as the impression gradually filters through to her conscious mind, she may wonder vaguely, 'Where have I heard that said before?'... Some things come as an inner knowing, an inner awareness... But we can esponge the memory so completely that the medium recalls nothing. It is like pulling down a shutter.

Jane Roberts, in talking of the process of Seth coming through her to dictate the book *Seth Speaks*, describes what she experiences during the trance state:

> I have certain unique experiences during sessions that seem to compensate for my lack of conscious creative involvement. Often I participate in Seth's great energy and humour, enjoying a sense of emotional richness and encountering Seth's personality on a very strange level. I feel his mood and vitality clearly, though they are not directed at me, but to whomever Seth is addressing at the moment. I feel them as they pass through me... I've had several 'out-of-body' experiences also during sessions, when I saw events actually happening some thousands of miles away.

J. Z. Knight, who channels Ramtha, is aware of not being around when Ramtha is through, and describes herself as going to 'his house' — in other words, the level of reality that he comes from. She feels that she has been doing a lot of learning on some other level, but she is not conscious of specific details. However, she knows the knowledge is stored in her subconscious, and at times she is aware of knowing things of which she had no previous awareness.

It's interesting that in Western society, trance is still looked at with much scepticism by the majority of people, and although it is beginning to be accepted a little more — mostly due to the Shirley MacLaines of the world — it is still a subject which the media goes to great lengths to disprove. However, in so-called primitive societies, it is not only acceptable, but highly honourable to be in touch with the psychic senses and to be able to use these faculties, trancing included, for the benefit of others.

In the parapsychology book *Psychic Exploration* compiled by former astronaut, Egdar D. Mitchell, there is a passage by Jean Houston, a psychologist who is director of the Foundation for Mind Research, near New York City. This passage talks about the attitude to children in these other cultures, and how their abilities are encouraged and indeed trained toward further use.

'Primitive cultures' are often much wiser than we are in dealing with those who reject the reality-consensus. A child in these so-called primitive cultures who shows a special faculty for seeing visions or for having psychic sensibility may be given rigorous training in different ways of seeing and being and then may grow up to be a critical member of the society — a priest, shaman, or prophet; a healer; or an artist. By contrast, too often in our society such children are intercepted by well-meaning 'guidance counsellors' and 'delivered' from their curious talent by teachers, psychiatrists, and other executors of the 'norm'. Thus do we continually cut off at the root a dynamic vehicle for society's well-being, a vehicle of inspiration, of ecstasy, and of entrance into the larger reality in which we all love and breathe but are conditioned out of seeing.

A few years back a distraught mother came to my husband and me with an eight-year-old child who had been branded by his headmaster as a potential juvenile delinquent. The school psychologist had washed his hands of the boy, and the child had refused to go back to the psychiatrist because he (the doctor) would only speak to the mother and wouldn't speak to him directly. So far he hadn't been forced into taking drugs to calm his behaviour, but that was only due to caring parents who felt there must be something that could be done for their child other than sedating him.

From all accounts that we had heard, we had been expecting a little monster. In fact the boy was not only one of the most beautiful-looking children I had ever seen, he was also highly intelligent (although always bottom of his class) and incredibly sensitive to everything going on around him. He was a bit like a psychic sponge: he would 'pick up' anything, including emotions belonging to other people, and would often be filled with totally irrational anger that he would take out on anyone close to him at the time.

Apart from the little healing we gave to him, we spent much of the time just talking with him and explaining what was actually happening to him on the non-physical level. Despite his age, his understanding was amazing, and his ability as a healer was already in evidence. So, against all logical, rational treatment for a kid of his age, we taught him how to protect himself against outside influences, how to meditate to keep more in touch with himself, and how to use his healing ability constructively.

At the end of the next school term his report read: 'If he keeps up such good work he will be a very useful member of the class'. According to his parents, he was a completely different child around the home — loving, more communicative, and far less aggressive.

This brings me back to the way we in the West seem to discourage the manifestation of psychic ability or sensitivity, and yet a far greater proportion of people in other parts of the world use and respect those who work in trance. For example, in cultures as varied as Indonesian, South American, South African and Haitian, some form of ritualistic trance is used by their healers, shamans or witchdoctors, either as part of their rites or in some method of healing or initiation.

What is trance work or mediumship used for in our society? Apart from the channelling of information mentioned in previous chapters, there are specific uses for this type of ability, especially in places like the UK where there is a strong spiritualist tradition.

One of the best known of all British mediums was Doris Stokes — a psychic who travelled all over the world in order to help people get in contact with friends and relatives who were deceased. These so-called dead people were still 'alive' in the spirit world and able to communicate through a trained sensitive, and as a result bring hope and joy to many.

As a child Doris Stokes had always been able to 'see' things that other people couldn't; for example, she saw the spirit body of a person who had just been killed walking beside the dead body — it took her quite a while to understand what was happening. It wasn't till her father died and she was able to communicate with him that she realised her gift, and actually started using it. It gave her courage and hope when she had been officially informed that her husband had been killed in the war. At the height of her grief her father 'visited' her and told her that her husband was still alive and would return, but only a little later warned her that her baby son would die. Both these predictions came true, and she learned to trust whatever her father communicated to her, even though the end result often brought intense pain.

At the age of 29 Doris Stokes took an exam set by the Spiritualist Union of Great Britain, and on passing became a recognised medium, entitled to work in any Spiritualist church in the country. At times she would be working on platforms in these churches, and would be so inundated with 'voices' in her ear that she would be hard-pressed to distinguish what was being said, and for whom. With experience she learnt to tell whether the voice was male or female, young or old, and so on, and then she would repeat to her audience what she was hearing. She would call out a name, and then tell that particular person that she had a message for them. It would often bring tears to the eyes of the person concerned to hear that his/her child/lover/parent was well and happy, and still loved them.

Doris Stokes saw her work as a medium as being the passing on of information from dead relatives and friends, to prove they lived in another dimension. However, some mediums are also pre-cognitive: that is, they have the ability to discern the future, often mistakenly referred to as clairvoyance, which is the ability to 'see' on another level.

At one time in her life Doris Stokes was warned by another medium of a serious illness. In her book *Voices in My Ear* she describes how a friend told her about a forthcoming problem which would result in her being hospitalised. 'They'll say you're going to die, but your father wants you to write this down. It's the name of the person you must ask for.' Sure enough, at the time predicted, she went into hospital, and, in agonising pain, heard the doctors tell her husband that she was dying. At that stage her husband remembered the warning, and got out the piece of paper with the name on it. Enquiries solicited that this particular person was a specialist in the field, so in the face of all warnings, Doris Stokes was transferred to another hospital, and she not only survived the journey, but she recovered.

Not all mediums are accurate all of the time, especially with regard to time, for it seems as if time is man-made. In the other dimension, time, as we know it doesn't exist. Invariably, I hear people say that so-and-so was really good as regards content, 'but her timing was all out'. Frequently I've been aware that something will happen, but if I try to enquire when, the answer is always the same: 'when the time is right'.

Taking what Doris Stokes does a step further are the mediums who allow the dead people to come through and talk directly to those they've left behind. One of the most fascinating examples of this was recorded by a South African judge, Jasper Swain, in his book *On the Death of my Son*. His son Mike, who had just left school, was killed very suddenly in an automobile accident. The father was totally devastated, angry, confused and full of grief. He received a telephone message from one of his old clients which read: 'As you once helped her in life, she will now help you in death'. Although he couldn't remember her, and his original reaction was one of anger, he eventually found the pressure in his mind so intense that he visited her.

As soon as he arrived the woman went into trance, and much to the judge's amazement he heard himself being addressed in a manner that only his dead son had ever used. He deliberately set out to try and trap this 'imposter', but at the end of an hour, when the lady came to herself, he made an appointment to come back with his bereaved wife and remaining son. Stunned by what had happened, he returned to the medium with his family that very same afternoon. Immediately she went into trance again, and once again Mike came through. This time they all asked questions to their hearts' content, and finally they asked for details of the accident. This is what Mike told them through the medium:

> I see a black car coming towards us. As it approaches us, I see this other car coming behind it. I can see this other car clearly because it is in the middle of the road, trying to pass the black car... The sun is glaring into the windscreen of the black car, and reflecting back into my eyes. I can see nothing but a bright silver radiance. It is blinding me. All of a sudden, the radiance changes from silver to gold. I am being lifted up into the air, out through the top of the car...

[He describes the same thing happening to his passenger, then continues:] We have been lifted thirty feet above the mini. And in one horrifying second, I see the little mini and this large car collide head-on. There is a noise like the snapping of steel banjo strings. The little mini bounces right off the highway, right over onto the gravel verge. It is finally brought to a halt in a cloud of dust when it hits a giant anthill... We now descend beside the mini. We see two crumpled bodies lying in it. We feel vaguely sorry that this thing should have happened to them. And we both fully understand that we are now, so far as mortals are concerned, dead.

Having heard these details, there was no doubting the authenticity of the person speaking through the voice of the medium. Mike then held a conversation with his family showing how aware he'd been of each person in the days since his death, and how he would be with them, for a while at any rate, to help them through the difficult times. Then he went on to explain the movement between the physical world and the spirit realm:

I can't say exactly how long it took us to leave the earth plane. It was much like flipping a radio dial from one station to another. When you turn the knob, you take for granted that another station will be awaiting your pleasure; you don't think there's anything unusual about it. That was how we moved from your world to our new one... when I need to regress myself back to your world, I have to reduce my vibrations to their slowest rate. This isn't easy, some of it is downright painful. It's like putting on a strait-jacket. I have to constrict myself more and more, like the rabbit in *Alice in Wonderland*, until my vibrations are moving as slowly as yours... I would say that ninety-five per cent of the souls at this level are completely unable to manifest at the earth level. Maybe in moments of urgency they can appear momentarily to their loved ones on earth, but they wouldn't promise to guarantee it.

Maybe this helps to explain why there appear to be so many souls prepared to give messages through the Doris Stokes of the world, and so few who actually come back to talk, with total confidence, via an authentic medium.

Many years ago the child of a friend of mine died from a rare disease. The mother was devastated, and naturally spent much time in grieving, a process very necessary for us on the physical level. Unknown to her I sat with a reliable trance channel and the child came through. He was incredibly happy that after a lifetime, short though it was, there was no longer any suffering from any of his physical handicaps, and he could run and play with other kids to his heart's content. 'Please tell Mummy not to keep crying so much', he said, 'It makes it difficult for me to go and be with the others. She keeps pulling me back and I need to be free to go.' He also sent messages of love, and asked after the family dog who had been a special friend.

This response to grieving seems to be fairly universal. Mike Swain, via the medium, puts it like this:

When you grieve for someone you love, your sorrow is immediately transmitted to him in his new world — a most beautiful world — but he cannot come back to the earth plane to comfort his mourners... This puts him in a hell of a quandary — he is torn between a desire to comfort his loved ones, knowing it to be impossible, and a need to adjust himself to his bright new surroundings.

So please tell those who are still on earth not to grieve for those of us who have come over here. I know it's impossible to ask them to rejoice; yet we on this side rejoice when an old friend comes here. I would ask the bereaved to sit and think of their loved ones instead of themselves. They will soon forget their own sorrows. Tell them, please, just to send their love and kindly thoughts for a calm journey and happy arrival, for the friend they have lost is already secure in this world of warmth and happiness.

Send wave upon wave of love. This will help the newly dead to stabilise, because it convinces them of the validity of both spheres of existence.

From a healing point of view it is really important that the person left behind is able to release the pain and grief of losing a loved one. It's good to be able to understand the process from the other perspective as well, and maybe the knowledge of what is actually happening to the loved one can help to lighten some of the grief.

One of the most moving sessions I can remember was with a mother who had lost her brain-damaged baby. The session was in three parts: first of all working on the loss itself; then on understanding the connection with a particular past life; then communication with the spirit of the dead baby, originally with myself mediating, and ultimately with the mother talking directly to the spirit. It was a very profound and moving experience for all concerned.

If all channelling for mediumship were of the calibre that I have talked about in this chapter, then there would be many people in this world who would not only lose their fear of death, but would also find their lives becoming more meaningful and fulfilling in a variety of ways. Of course there are charlatans about, and unfortunately the innocent are the most vulnerable to these people. However, the intention is paramount: if you have a clear intention to receive help from the highest level, and you only trust what resonates within you at a deep level, then the chances are you will draw to you that which is good and true, and maybe your life will change as a result.

Chapter Five

The Multiplicity of Spirit Communications

Spirits make connections with us in a wide variety of ways. Some of the more common ways are through the medium of psychometry, astrology and the tarot; through spiritual readings and counsellings; through psychic artistry; and through music.

In many countries there are people whose work involves the giving of channelled counselling/readings to those in need. Some of these readings come from tuning in to the psychic senses, while many others are from people able to tune in to a higher energy and channel this energy in whatever way is appropriate.

The person searching should have a clear intention of contacting as high and as pure a source as possible, and if this intention is there, there is less likelihood of being led astray. Even though I recommend people to be in contact with their own inner guidance or divinity within, there are sometimes occasions when outside energy or another's viewpoint can be of benefit.

It is very hard to discriminate between the use of psychic senses and the use of channelled information for this type of work. What mostly seems to happen is somewhere between the two. I have watched and felt the gradual merging of these two energies, and it's as if the use of the psychic energy lays the path for tuning in to a higher energy, and the flow-on is a natural progression.

A very talented psychometrist friend of mine will pick up an oject belonging to a client, and will immediately launch into a reading about the person who owns the object. She tunes in to the energy vibrations of the object (psychometry), initially using her psychic senses to do this. However, as she proceeds deeper into the reading, her crown *chakra* becomes activated and the energy can be 'seen' as a clear band of light flowing into the top of her head. As this happens, the quality of her speech and of the information coming through starts to change in a subtle manner.

She is amazingly accurate about both past events and the present situation in people's lives, and gives very clear pointers as to how people can help themselves. She never takes away the free will of the person concerned, but she does make suggestions about the direction in which they should proceed to bring greater fulfilment into their lives.

Psychometry can be a powerful tool for a change. A good psychometrist can be so accurate, even regarding details of very early childhood, that it is possible to trigger someone into releasing deep-seated physical and emotional blocks. The way that psychometry works is quite logical: an object, like a person, is made up of molecules of energy, and this energy is tangible to some people. Tuning in to this energy, whether directly that of the person or the energy of an object belonging to the person, can lead to amazing results. It is possible to tell a person's whole physical and emotional make-up, the state of their energy centres or *chakras*, their past, and also their probable future.

Psychometry is sometimes classified as a form of fortune-telling, but it can also be a powerful adjunct to healing and should not be dismissed lightly. It is basically a simple technique to learn; it has a lot to do with trust and feeling, and I have seen unskilled/trainee psychometrists tap in to areas totally unknown to them about their 'clients', leading to far-reaching results. I find that tuning in to a client the first time he or she comes for a consultation is invaluable. Not only do I hear what the person perceives the problem to be on a superficial level, but I also develop my own sense of what is happening on an energy level as well as on the emotional level.

There are also many other people who utilise a key, as psychometrists utilise an object, to help them tune in to their clients. Probably the largest number come under the heading of astrologers. Although astrology is scientifically based, many of the really good astrologers seem to take it a step further. These people allow the knowledge gained from looking at the chart to lead them into very detailed information, often achieved through channelling (sometimes without their conscious knowledge of this fact). To begin with they will read the chart in a conventional and scientific way, but from then on, the interpretation varies considerably from astrologer to astrologer. With some, it stays very much in the realm of what can be learnt from study, but with others, an indefinable quality comes in. A certain depth and awareness that over-steps the boundaries of 'normal' astrological interpretation becomes apparent, and the person receiving the reading is often deeply touched.

Apart from astrologers, there are also people who use numerology as their key, and others who use the tarot cards. These are subjects that can be studied and learnt, and yet still leave plenty of room for individual interpretation. The practitioners whom I know to be uncannily accurate on many levels are obviously highly intuitive, but invariably many of these are channelling from another dimension as well as using the tools of numerology or tarot cards.

An example of this is a young woman I know who starts off doing a tarot reading in the conventional manner, and then half-way through the reading she spontaneously goes into trance. The tarot acts as her bridge to another level, and through it, she is able to give some thought-provoking, and indeed transformational, sessions. The people with whom she works are frequently amazed at the accuracy of her information, and many comment that they have never had a reading like it before.

There are also a number of psychic practitioners who give even more specific counsellings, such as in-depth advice on guides, current blockages, state of the *chakras* and so on. The worldwide organisation known as the Inner Peace Movement (IPM) is one such group that specialises in these detailed spiritual counsellings. The goal of IPM is to help people become more in charge of their lives, and better able to make decisions based on using the universal energy, through the medium of their spiritual helpers or guides.

The IPM has an extensive list of the different counsellings or profiles that it gives, but the first one an individual receives is the orientation profile. This is a counselling to help the searcher become more aware of his/her guides. The information is channelled from the guidance of a trained counsellor, and thence imparted to the person concerned. The profile goes into a fair amount of detail about the guides and why they are there, and as well, the counsellor will teach communication between the individual and his/her inner guidance.

There are also many people who tune in to the guides of the person asking for the reading, and provide information from this source. Sometimes it can be amazingly accurate, down to the tiniest detail that the person channelling could not possibly have known. But there are also cases when the information is coming from the subconscious, or even the ego, of the counsellor, and this can lead to misunderstanding and pain. For example, a woman came to me desperately upset because she had been told by a renowned channel that she had not only failed to achieve her life purpose, but that she never would achieve it. In that woman's mind, what was the point of going on living?

Another disturbing story involves a young girl scheduled to go away on an overseas trip with a friend. The friend went to a psychic who claimed to channel from the person's guides, and was told not to buy her ticket as the young woman would be dead by the time of the departure date. This advice was quite blatant; no reasons were given, just a clear statement of what proved to be totally false. However, the suffering and mental anguish that those two girls went through in the interim was indescribable.

Another totally unethical form of behaviour is manipulation: 'My/your guides have told me that you will be working with me' or 'will be giving me a certain sum of money', or whatever — not very subtle, but you would be surprised at the number of people who have fallen into this trap. I know that we create our own reality, but dealing with manipulation is an uncomfortable lesson that many have had to learn.

I find it very hard when people report to me what a particular channel is supposed to have said, and ask me for my thoughts about it. I can only answer that it's none of my business, and suggest that they focus on what they themselves really FEEL on a deep level about what has come through. The answer must come back to their own gut reaction, although if someone desperately wants to hear something specific, then it's harder to be objective about it. This is where it is so important to be in tune with one's own inner being, and to trust what feels right at the time. I find it can be really positive if I say something to someone which causes him/her to resonate so strongly that he/she bursts into tears. It means the words have struck a chord at a very deep level, and this is the sort of resonance I am talking about. Such a response happens frequently with good counsellors, therapists and healers.

I remember, many years ago now, being with an excellent medium who had spent years counselling and helping people from all walks of life. She had told me many things that resonated perfectly, and that felt right. However, there were a couple of 'misfits' that I just couldn't connect with on any level, and no matter what I wanted to believe, they just did not resonate anywhere. After trying for a while to make sense of them, I forgot about them until many years later when it so happened that events in my life gave proof to what I had felt. They had been totally inaccurate statements which, had I believed and acted upon them, might have caused quite a few problems for me, yet the rest of what had been said was totally accurate. I can't explain how or why it is possible for such a discrepancy to exist, but I've come across it time and again — especially in areas which are very difficult to prove, such as past lives, future lives, and details about guides.

Past lives is an area that has caused so much controversy that it's worth briefly mentioning here. (I'll go into greater detail in Chapter 7.) Unfortunately, past lives have become fashionable in society today. It's possible to have such a thing as a past-life reading where a theoretically skilled or trained counsellor will tell you a list of past lives which may or may not be relevant to you today. Many of these people are quite genuine and indeed do have some skill, and what they say resonates to the person concerned, and maybe helps them understand what is happening in his or her life. However, such knowledge doesn't seem to change anything, and I've noticed that many people tend to grasp on to little details and then bring them up as justification for what they're currently doing.

Somehow, it's lost all proportion, and people are getting led astray by what their imagination wants to hear. I feel very strongly about this issue, because for many years I specialised in past life therapy as an aspect of wholistic healing, and I often had clients who had been told something that was blatantly inaccurate. It was rare that in the course of therapy someone would actually re-live a life they had been 'told' about. Even rarer was the person who had experienced a life as a world-famous personage, and yet quite a few are told that they were individuals such as Cleopatra or Henry the Eighth.

A totally different type of channelling comes through certain people in the form of paintings. Known as psychic artists, these people are often very talented artistically, and once they have learnt to channel a whole new dimension is opened up to them, allowing them to incorporate their new-found spiritual energy into their physical skills.

One form this can take is when the artist channels pictures of guides belonging to the person who has come for the sitting. There is no real proof that it is not just a pleasant portrait from the imagination of the artist, but invariably there is such a strong resonance (with a tuned-in artist, that is) that there is little room for doubt. A well-known Melbourne artist springs to mind: Marion Ruffin had been trained in fine arts, and it wasn't until she started sitting in a mediumship development and healing circle that these significant pictures started appearing. Although trained to bring through pictures of loved ones and relatives, she finds that her strongest channel is connected with spirit guides. She give a very individual stamp to all of her pictures, and I've seen many over the years. The majority of her clients have resonated with their drawings.

I had an interesting experience when she did one for me. I showed the picture to two friends with whom I had done a lot of work. They both instantly recognised the being as someone who would occasionally work through me. When that would happen, my face would apparently change shape, and according to one of them, I would become masculine-looking and entirely different in appearance. My friend had commented on this more than once, and as the face in the picture was an elderly, male American Indian, it was hardly surprising that I would look different!

As Marion Ruffin draws, she gives details as to the connection between the guide and the client, and what they are here to do in that partnership. She also channels messages from the spirit being, and these can take the form of guidance, information, and understanding of the life of the person concerned.

Another psychic artist is Coral Polge, the world-famous British artist renowned for her portraits of those in the spirit world. Over the years she has painted numerous pictures which have both delighted and amazed sitters everywhere. She combines her artistic talent and training with the skills of mediumship, and transmits onto paper the spirit with whom she is communicating. Invariably it is a relative or loved one of the person sitting for her, although sometimes old photographs have to be unearthed to prove the fact. Occasionally the picture is not for the sitter, but for a friend or acquaintance that the artist has never even met.

During a demonstration at Stanstead Hall in England, Coral Polge drew a picture of a seventeen-year-old boy who had been killed in a motor cycle accident. He was desperate to get in touch with his mother, about whom he was worried, and also his sick father. He had obviously passed over only a few days previously, and was still very tied to the earth plane — hence his concern about his parents being upset at the accident.

No-one in the audience recognised the boy, or the name Fred, which the artist kept hearing. Suddenly the wife of a Spiritualist minister spoke up. She said that a few days previously her husband had taken the funeral service of a boy killed in a motor cycle accident. Although she had never met the boy, she was sure that his name wasn't Fred, but Andrew Weston. However, after the demonstration the minister's wife took the portrait and passed it on to Andrew's parents, just in case. The likeness was unmistakable, and it was later discovered that the boy's father used the nickname 'Fred' for his son!

Originally, when Coral Polge combined her two considerable talents of art and mediumship, she would mostly draw spirit guides, and as she herself would say, there is no real proof of the reality of these portrayals. However, after a while, the first picture of a relative came through, and then she was advised by a well-known medium friend of hers to 'demand' a higher percentage of relatives. It meant sticking her neck out a bit further as the sitters could confirm or deny the existence of the people she drew. However, her confidence grew as the quality of her paintings improved, and gradually more and more relatives of sitters were attracted to her.

Being a medium also brings its share of problems when trying to draw someone who has passed over. Often the artist starts to draw someone who has died a traumatic death — they may have been injured in an accident — and when this happens, the memory of the suffering often gets in the way. The spirit person might start to look at the damage that was done, and the shock of that memory can actually break the link. Sometimes a spirit being will project him/herself as if from an earlier period of their life when he or she was without disfigurement, and this often makes it hard for the relatives to recognise the people concerned.

Possibly the hardest situation of all to cope with is when the artist/medium takes on characteristics of the spirit person. In the book *The Living Image* by Coral Polge and Kay Hunter, the artist talks about herself in relation to these problems: 'Sometimes my facial expressions must look extraordinary because I take on the features of the people I am drawing. I screw up my eyes or frown, and if drawing an old person I sometimes feel as though I have no teeth.'

On one occasion she was assailed by the last memories of someone who had committed suicide, something that can be both uncomfortable and even dangerous.

As I started to draw the girl I immediately began to feel light-headed. I could hear myself talking, but from a distance. 'I have a young lady here who died of something which made her feel very giddy, I feel as if I can't breathe — everything is floating away.' I began to cough, and felt that if I wasn't careful I was going to fall over on the platform because my head was swimming. I asked the girl in the spirit world not to come too close to me in case I collapsed. Whether I would actually have done so I'm not sure, but I felt as though I was being completely asphyxiated.

Afterwards it turned out that the portrait she had painted was of the daughter of a woman in the audience. The girl had died of carbon monoxide poisoning

Another artist in a similar field but with a slightly different slant is German-born Susi Wegner, now living in the Blue

Mountains of New South Wales. An accomplished artist whose paintings have a touch of magic and mystery, Susi Wegner for years painted pictures that delighted children and adults alike. After the conception of her third child, the quality of her paintings changed and somehow seemed to take on a new dimension. As she learnt to tune in to her own inner guidance, so too did this tuning in start to take place while she was painting. In time she realised what was happening: she was picking up the energy of the person who had commissioned the picture, and the end result was channelled from another level of reality into the physical. The pictures are painted in a variety of styles, being totally different from person to person, and while these pictures are coming through, Susi Wegner receives messages concerning the person, either to do with their life at the moment, a past life, or an issue that might be causing problems.

After completing a painting, Susi sits in meditation and allows the writing to flow for as long as necessary. Then, when the person comes to collect the finished picture, she reads out what she has written, sometimes adding more verbally, and helps the person to understand the depth of what has come through. Often this can be an emotional time for the owner of the picture as it can bring up issues and forgotten memories, but it is all part of the process, and many people have been helped considerably by this talented artist.

Another very different type of channel is Rosemary Brown, an English housewife who has spent many years of her life seemingly in communication with some of the greatest musical composers of history. She believes that the spirits of Liszt, Chopin, Beethoven, Debussy, Schumann, Bach, Rachmaninov and Brahms are using her to communicate music from another world.

Rosemary Brown had a background of comparatively humble circumstances, fraught with poverty and the battle to make ends meet. This was intensified by the death of her beloved husband, and for a while life was a real struggle. She had to take any menial job she could in order to support her two children, and there was certainly never enough money at any stage in her life for her to train for a lifetime of music. In fact, the first few piano lessons she had were from the man who played the piano for the local ballroom-dancing class.

After a while she changed teachers, but the piano at her home had many keys that didn't play, and as there was no electricity in her home, and the room she practised in rarely had a fire to warm it, often there were times when her fingers were too cold and stiff to be able to practise. Her piano lessons lasted only a year or so, as they were the first economy she had to make in a financial emergency. Later she received another year of piano lessons, and together that was the sum total of Rosemary Brown's musical training.

As a child she was always psychically gifted, and would see spirits of the so-called dead. At the age of seven, she saw Franz Liszt for the first time, standing at her bedside. At that stage he didn't introduce himself, but he did say that when she grew up, he would come back and give her music. That was all. However, the experience was very real to the child, and she never forgot him or what he said, even though she had no comprehension of what it meant or who he was.

It was many years later that he came back to fulfil his promise. Today, he is the leader of a group of famous composers who visit Rosemary Brown regularly, and give her new compositions for the world to hear. The work involved in this has been tremendous, especially as she had no formal training in music and the technicalities involved, and she certainly had no idea how to orchestrate.

One of the interesting aspects of Rosemary Brown's work is the question of why the music was transmitted in the first place. Maybe the best answer to this is in the book *Unfinished Symphonies* by Rosemary Brown, and comes from Sir Donald Tovey, a distinguished musician and composer who died in 1940. Using the same channel as the composers, he transmitted these words:

> We are not transmitting music to Rosemary Brown simply for the sake of offering pleasure in listening thereto; it is the implications relevant to this phenomena which we hope will stimulate sensible and sensitive interest and stir many who are intelligent and impartial to consider and explore the

unknown regions of man's mind and psyche.

When man has plumbed the mysterious depth of his veiled consciousness, he will then be able to soar to correspondingly greater heights.

Following on from this explanation is the question, from Rosemary Brown's point of view, as to why she was the person chosen for the task. The answer comes from Liszt: 'Because you volunteered. Long before you were born . . . You agreed to be the link between us and the world when you were in another aspect of your life'. Why then was Rosemary Brown not put in a situation where she could have had intense musical training? Again Liszt answers: 'You have sufficient training for our purposes. Had you been given a really full musical education it would have caused you to acquire too many ideas and theories of your own. These would have been an impediment to us'.

As a result of publicity about the music she channels, Rosemary Brown has been the subject of much investigation. Her words and music are constantly being analysed and she has taken tests of every different variety: musical tests, intelligence tests, pyschological tests, psychic tests, and even apparently totally irrelevant tests. In most cases the music is proven to be totally compatible with the style of the specific composer, but the sceptics continually try to furnish some other explanation as to the true source. In fact, one musician suggested that she had actually received prolonged and advanced musical training, and then suffered amnesia, causing her to forget this fact. Her family doctor soon put the facts straight, and many people can vouchsafe other details of her life as well.

Anyone knowledgeable about music realises that Rosemary Brown would have had to be a musical genius not only to have composed and recorded so many different pieces of music, but to have written them in at least a dozen different styles. In 1971, some mechanical tests using a computer were applied to the music received from the spirits — in order to analyse and assess the music. The musicologist and mathematician in charge of the computer, Stan Kelly, punched up paper tapes representing random samples of music written by Liszt, Chopin and Beethoven during their lifetimes. Then he punched up tapes transmitted to the channel by the same composers. The evidence evinced by the use of this technique indicated strong correlation, especially with Chopin. (This didn't surprise Rosemary Brown as she feels that Chopin seems the most capable of communicating music clearly and quickly). The computer expert said that scores of over sixty are sufficient to show correlation. The scores obtained were in the eighties and nineties!

What is interesting to note is that the handwriting on the manuscripts and the way the notes are written down vary between the pieces from the different composers, 'almost as if I were being guided when writing down the music', says Rosemary Brown. She likens the process to automatic writing, and feels that in transmitting the music, there could be some form of automatic writing involved. Sometimes the composers actually move her hands over the keys, and sometimes they just talk to her and she has to write what she hears — not an easy task when the person doesn't know how to write music properly in the first place.

A final anecdote about Rosemary Brown will illustrate a tangible and practical use of her ability to communicate with these composers. The musician and composer, Richard Rodney Bennett, was due to give a piano recital of Debussy music, and was worried about the interpretation of one of the pieces. All he mentioned was the name Debussy, but not which pieces he was planning to play, or which one he was concerned about. Debussy himself was apparently delighted the recital was taking place, and gave Rosemary Brown a long, detailed description of how the piece that was bothering the musician should be tackled. He went into it quite thoroughly, describing various passages, and saying which ones needed more pedal, and which chords should be staccato, and so on. This is what Rosemary Brown said about the incident:

It was really extraordinary because I had been given no indication at all about which piece of music was involved, and when I told Richard Rodney Bennett, he said: 'That's very strange, because everything you have said could apply to the piece of music I'm concerned with. In fact, I don't think it could apply to any other piece of Debussy's'.

He did, in fact, follow the advice given by Debussy and found that it solved the problem.

A totally different type of channelling is worth mentioning here, although is cannot really be classified under any heading I have used so far. I call it a visual, hand communication, and it is a channelled experience more than anything else. It is a series of incredibly beautiful hand movements that speak to the heart of the watcher, and can mean something different for everyone who sees it. It is filled with fluid motion accompanied by a strong presence of love energy, and seems to touch all who observe it, although many do not actually understand it with their heads. It feels rather like a blend of Egyptian, Indian and Tai Chi movements, and for me, it is triggered by the sun in nature, although on rare occasions I have channelled it indoors.

All these different types of channelling are valid in that they touch the person concerned, and many people have been, and will continue to be, helped in a variety of ways. Obviously, not all methods suit each person, but once you are prepared to trust your own feeling, then you will feel yourself being drawn toward the method which is appropriate for you.

Chapter Six

Channelling for the Release of Spirit Possession

Possession in spiritual terms means the invasion by a spirit of a physical body. In other words, it is the taking over of someone's living body by a spirit being which also once had a physical body. Possession does exist: we cannot close our eyes to this fact, much as we may like to, but it is not usually associated with the dramatic and terrifying events portrayed in movies. Such movies are produced for entertainment (if this can be called entertaining) and for the horror and shock value.

Possession unfortunately takes place far more often than one would imagine, but it need not happen at all in many instances. It can be prevented, and it can certainly be dealt with. It is most commonly connected with spirits who are here to cause trouble, but it can also happen that a spirit is hovering out of love. In the latter situation, though it is technically called possession due to possible adverse effects, it is relatively easy to persuade the possessing entity to withdraw once the effects have been explained to it.

Many years ago when I was still in the early stages of learning about healing, a friend came to my husband and me in great distress. This man, whom I shall call Grant, explained that on various occasions, usually when he was in a stressful situation, he suffered the symptoms equivalent to a stroke — intense pain in his head, and progressively worsening hemiplegia or paralysis down one side. He had seen countless doctors, undergone brain scans, and received all the usual tests available for someone in that condition. They had all proved negative. The final straw was to be told that his problem was psychosomatic, and that he would either have to learn to live with it (difficult when trying to maintain a high-level banking position) or take strong tranquillisers for the rest of his life.

Physically, mentally and emotionally Grant seemed to be in excellent health — other than on the occasions he suffered the symptoms discussed — so we decided to tackle the problem from a different viewpoint. I tuned in to him in a less conventional way than the medical profession would have done, and sensed with him a presence which I proceeded to describe. As the details unfolded, his expression changed from one of simple interest to one of total amazement. Apparently the person I was describing was his grandmother with whom he had lived as a child and who had died when he was eleven years old. They had been very close, and as he obviously grieved heavily for her, she had 'hung around', wishing to help him as much as possible. Unfortunately, she didn't realise that what she was really doing was manifesting her last memory of this life — a stroke and the subsequent hemiplegia prior to her death.

Once this was explained to the spirit of the grandmother, she left, saddened, but understanding why it was necessary. To this day, Grant has never suffered a recurrence of the symptoms, and this experience was well over a decade ago.

What is the connection between possession and channelling? To me, channelling is the simplest and least painful method of accomplishing the release of a possessing entity. This release is commonly termed psychic rescue or soul release, although in religious terms it is known as exorcism, and is considered a dangerous occupation.

The most successful method I have found is for two people to work together, one to channel the entity which is possessing the person, and the other to communicate verbally with it and to 'channel the light' to it. This method takes into consideration the fact that the entity also has a right to exist, and a choice can be given. This choice is whether the entity departs willingly, to go to the light — the level of spiritual existence — or whether light energy is sent so that it penetrates and surrounds the being, forcing it to depart to the relevant level where it can be helped. Destruction I cannot condone, and although some groups are ruthless in their methods, I don't believe in 'strong-arm' tactics. I also don't go along with those who happily get the entity out of that particular human being, but then leave it floating around in the ethers, ready to pounce on the next unsuspecting candidate for possession.

In the book *Reaching for the Other Side*, the author Dawn Hill explains the process that takes place in release work:

It should be remembered that the technique of psychic rescue requires the medium to draw an entity into his own aura. It is a form of carefully controlled possession. While the medium is in a trance he is dependent upon the expertise of the control, who works in conjunction with the spirit guides to ease the entity through his aura and into the spiritual sphere to which it belongs. A mistake on the part of the control can break the spiritual contact, leaving the entity enmeshed in the medium's aura and capable of controlling the entranced physical body. Since some of these entities are malicious and violent, the results could be tragic.

Psychic rescue usually takes place for one of two reasons. The first concerns a situation where the entity is earthbound and is literally a lost and/or confused soul, often as a result of having died suddenly and traumatically. There is usually no concept of the fact that he or she is dead. When this is the case, our job is to explain as gently as possible to the spirit, what has happened. As Dawn Hill says: 'Earthbound entities are not evil fiends; they are human souls in need of help'.

I recently worked with a pathetic case of a drunken sailor. Quite unwittingly he had been giving a hard time to a young girl, and when he started speaking through the body of the medium, he was craving a drink. He wouldn't believe me when I told him that the physical body he was talking through wasn't his. He laughed, and reckoned that I must be the drunken one! When I helped him realise that he was in a female body, he became frantic for his drink, and wouldn't believe me when I said we had none in the house. He was all for getting up and rummaging in the cupboards. After a bit of explaining, he eventually got the message, but I couldn't help laughing when I inadvertently mentioned the word 'spirits'. That meant only one thing to him! Finally, he withdrew gracefully, somewhat stunned by the feeling of the light energy, but happy to be going somewhere positive.

The other type of rescue or release is much harder: it is used in a situation where the possessing entity is specifically with a person for the purpose of causing them harm. There is usually a personal reason involved, such as a desire for power over the person, revenge, or a hex or curse, and the release in such circumstances can be a longer and more drawn-out process.

A case that comes to mind is one that involved a child, and was associated with revenge. The boy was ten years old at the time, and seemed unusually accident prone. However, instead of grazing his knees, cutting his hands or any other of the multitude of accidents that always seem to happen to children, his accidents all involved his head. He would fall either directly onto it, sometimes even becoming unconscious as a result, or he would be hit on the head, or bruise his face or chin. He never seemed to injure any other part of his body.

I was a bit concerned about allowing what could be a nasty entity through in front of a child — it's something I would not normally do — but his mother reassured me that he would be able to handle it. It seemed important for some reason that he should be aware of what had happened, and his mother stayed with him throughout the experience.

The personality that came through was one who had lived in Roman times when he and the boy had been friends and soldiers. Apparently the boy had lost his sword in battle and so took that belonging to his friend. As a result, the friend was unable to defend himself and was killed. So strong was his hatred and resentment toward the person he had thought his friend, that he determined to get his own back by trying to destroy him. It took quite a while for the entity to understand that he was holding himself back, but when he eventually left, it was of his own free will.

It was relatively gentle in retrospect, and the boy seemed to accept it all. Certainly he had no more accidents involving his head, and as the release took place many years ago now, it is safe to assume that the entity will not trouble him again.

So what is it that makes someone a target for a possessing entity? In cases such as those mentioned, it appears that the entity has been with the person since birth. However, there appears to be a pattern developing as to the type of person who has problems in this particular area. They can be people who are very depressed, often with a lot of deep-seated emotional trauma: people who are deeply troubled and confused, often in a state of fear, and people who are surrounded by negativity. These people need special help and counselling after a release has taken place. Without this, they tend to attract the same circumstance again, for it's as if the negative aspect inside them draws further negativity towards it.

Another likely candidate for possession might be a person who has been unconscious for a while, giving the entity a chance to enter into the body while there is no conscious control over it. (See the case of the heroin addict mentioned later in this chapter.) There are also people who like the attention that 'possessing an entity' seems to give them, and sometimes they use this 'entity' as an escape from taking responsibility for their lives. This can be taken to extremes in cases where people are scared to acknowledge their own shadow side, and what manifests as an entity is actually a thought form of a part of their own being.

Those who are heavily into drugs and alcohol are especially susceptible, as are those who play in areas they do not understand. These areas include the ouija board, black magic and so on. I will explain each in turn because it is important to understand the dangers involved, how they can be prevented, and how much extra work, and even danger, could be avoided if people only had a bit more knowledge and understanding about this topic

The ouija board is quite simply a device used as a focus for attracting the attention of spirits. What people don't seem to realise is the incredible danger in playing with this type of psychic tool. As soon as a group of people sit together with the intention of communicating with spirits, they make themselves wide open to any entities — malevolent as well as benevolent. This is so whether the whole group believes in what is taking place or is highly sceptical. Unless the members of the group know exactly what they are doing, the results can be very traumatic, to say the least.

I know a group of teenagers who thought it would be fun to hold a seance. Unfortunately they didn't tell me about it until afterwards, when it was too late. None of them had really believed that anything would happen, and when they received communication from a friend who had been killed in a motorcycle accident, they were shattered. They were so terrified by what happened that even now, some time later, one is still having recurrent nightmares. An ouija board is not a toy; it can be as dangerous as giving a box of matches to a child, and if I had my way, ouija boards would be banned.

Another, possibly even more dangerous field in which to play is that of black magic. I will discuss this area more fully in Chapter 9, but I would like to mention here that some of the nastiest entities, and some of the hardest work I've ever had to do, have resulted from situations in which people either foolishly became involved with the black, or have had a hex or curse put on them by someone with black knowledge.

In fact the very first release I ever watched was the result of a witchdoctor's curse in South Africa. An English friend of my husband and myself, Ralph, used to live in South Africa, and at one stage he accidentally ran foul of the local witchdoctor. When threatened by him, Ralph laughed, and the witch-doctor had proceeded to place a full curse upon him. Not believing in this type of ritual magic, Ralph thought nothing of it.

A few years later, when sitting in a healing and development group, he spontaneously entered a trance-like state. His stature seemed to grow, both in height as well as width, and his nose became negroid-looking. The entity that came through banged on the arms of the chair in which he was sitting, and in a loud voice, kept saying: 'I'm big and I'm black; I'm big and I'm black'. There is no way that any of us in the room would have physically been a match for him. The end result was that the lady in charge of the group channelled a strong light being who was able to 'fight' the possessing entity, and finally facilitate its removal. We were all left in a state of shock, Ralph most of all! After that he took great care never to cross anyone, anywhere, and spent the next few years learning all he could about a wide variety of healing modalities, mind power and positive thinking.

More recently, and closer to home, was an incident where a client was cursed quite openly by an acquaintance of his. The man wanted to end a brief relationship, and the woman involved was furious. She warned him that if he did finish with her, he would never have another day's good luck in his life. Of course he didn't believe her and went on his way without thinking twice about it. The very next day he was involved in a serious car accident which put him off the road for a few months. As a result he was off work for a long period of time, and this in turn led to financial difficulties.

The entity that was channelled was the spirit of a woman well versed in the arts of black magic. She was most derogatory toward me, accusing me of working with a local priest — who, we since discovered, campaigns heavily against the black — and of being one of his 'religious, idealistic wimps'. The insults kept coming for a considerable length of time, and it wasn't until she finally had to draw breath that I was able to get a word in. Talking to her did no good at all, so eventually I started sending the light to her, but she was as well defended against the light as I was against the black, so we reached a stalemate.

Knowing we had to reach a conclusion somehow, I asked for inspiration, and as a result, started talking to her about her childhood. The next thing I knew I was putting a teddy bear into her arms, and she burst into tears! Not the usual action during a release, but it had the desired effect. After that it was simply a matter of letting her feel the difference that love in its true essence made, rather than clinging onto the anger and hate she had grown up with. She left willingly after that, and the man was free to start putting his life back together.

Alcohol is another huge problem in today's society. Not only is it freely available to all and sundry, but it is also highly addictive, and can lead to a breakdown in both physical and mental health. If a person is in a negative or depressed frame of mind, then he or she will automatically draw negative energy. If, on top of this, the physical is lowered through excessive alcohol or drug abuse, then the so-called spiritual protective sheath or aura (said to be an electro-magnetic field surrounding all things) seems to fade or split open.

In his book *Return From Tomorrow*, Dr George Ritchie, a practising psychiatrist, describes a series of events he experienced during 9 minutes when he was pronounced clinically dead. One of these led him, in his non-physical form (or astral form, as he described it) to look into a bar. All physical patrons were surrounded by their auras, but there were also many non-physical beings like himself, with no auras, and most were desperately trying to pick up a glass, but to no avail. In the words of Dr Ritchie: 'Their hands just passed straight through the tumblers. It was obvious that none of the patrons could see or feel these thirsty, disembodied beings.'

Dr Ritchie's experience occurred towards the close of the Second World War, and the bar was one much frequented by sailors on service leave. Dr Ritchie continues:

One very intoxicated sailor rose unsteadily from his stool and then fell heavily to the floor, unconscious. I was staring in amazement as the bright cocoon around him simply opened up. It parted at the crown of his head and began peeling away. Instantly, quicker than I'd ever seen anyone move, one of the insubstantial beings who had been standing at the bar was on top of him. In the next instant, to my mystification, the springing figure had vanished. It all happened even before the two men beside him had dragged the unconscious body from under their feet. One minute I'd distinctly seen two beings like myself, yet, by the time they'd propped the sailor up against the wall there was only one.

Watching it happen twice more, completely stupefied, Dr Ritchie goes on to surmise:

Presumably these substance-less creatures once had solid bodies as I myself had. Suppose that when they had been in these bodies they had developed a dependence on alcohol that went beyond the physical. That became mental. Spiritual even. Then when they lost that body, except when they briefly could take possession of another one, they would be cut off for all eternity from the thing they could never stop craving.

The implications of this are far greater than might be perceived at first. From all such accounts, the sailor, and others like him, change in personality and habits, seemingly developing the personality and characteristics of the beings that enter them.

About ten years ago I worked with a teenage alcoholic who had tried everything available to him at the time, including Alcoholics Anonymous, but all conventional methods of help were to no avail. He persisted with the uncontrollable craving, Ultimately, he decided that psychic rescue, as a last resort, might help him. It turned out that he had four entities with him, three alcoholics craving for drink, and one drug addict craving a hit. Since that session, this former alcoholic has not only stopped drinking, but has also never displayed the slightest desire for alcohol.

According to Dr Carl Wickland in his book *30 Years Among the Dead*:

> Lacking physical bodies through which to carry out earthly propensities, many discarnate intelligences are attracted to the magnetic light which emanates from mortals, and, consciously or unconsciously, attach themselves to these magnetic auras, finding an avenue of expression through influencing, obsessing or possessing human beings. Such obtruding spirits influence susceptible sensitives with their thoughts, impart their own emotions to them, and weaken their will power and often control their actions, producing great distress, mental confusion and suffering....
>
> Relentless as is the grip which the drug habit holds on its mortal victims, the power of narcotics extends even more tyrannically beyond the grave. The desire is implanted in the very soul itself and the agony of earthbound spirits, whose cravings for gratification are in vain, is beyond description. Such spirits frequently obtain partial satisfaction through controlling mortal sensitives, and forcing them to become addicts of some drug.

I worked recently, with a heroin addict who had just started 'the methadone program'. He was very depressed and still finding life hard to come to terms with, as well as finding it almost impossible to shake off the craving. What had happened was that at the age of thirteen he had been hit on the head by an iron bar, and had fallen unconscious for 24 hours. Within six months of the accident he was using heroin. When he was in his twenties he had a similar accident involving his head. Some time afterwards he underwent the methadone program.

What we discovered was that he had been taken over by the spirit of a drug addict — an English-speaking hippie from the sixties who had been locked up in a tiny, cage-like prison in Afghanistan. Apparently he had bribed the gaolers to bring him heroin to enable him to survive the appalling conditions. The prison was like a cage in which animals are kept, and he was locked into it with other prisoners; none of them could even stand up straight owing to the size of the cage. Throughout the session my body was bent over as if feeling the physical restraint of these bars, and I found myself constantly scratching various parts of my body. I don't know whether this constant irritation was due to fleas in the Afghani gaol, or whether it had some connection with heroin symptoms.

Finally he could no longer stand the situation and the conditions, and he took an overdose to escape. However, even without a physical body he was still craving for a fix, so he attached himself to someone who was in a position to get one. This not only ensured that the unfortunate human being would be unlikely ever to break the habit, but also that he himself still felt caged. At the end of much discussion and explanation, he was finally persuaded to go to the light in order to be free from both the cage and the addiction. A few weeks later a friend, who had sat in on the session as a learning process, saw the addict again, and commented on how much better he looked, and how much lighter his energy was.

It seems as if drug abuse opens up the aura to invasion in much the same way that Dr Ritchie described with regard to the alcohol drinkers. Certainly many of the people who need this type of healing/rescue work have at some stage taken mind-altering drugs, such as marihuana, LSD or heroin. I don't believe that all people who have resorted to drugs are necessarily prone to psychic attack, but I do believe that people should become aware of the inherent dangers involved.

Sometimes a possession case can result from something that

under normal circumstances would be quite unremarkable. I mentioned in Chapter 5 that psychometry, the reading of objects, is an easy tool to facilitate tuning in to a person on a deep level. However, it can have side effects if not practised under controlled conditions.

I was once handed a brooch belonging to a man's wife, and was asked what I made of it. Without thinking twice I tuned into it (I wouldn't be so rash today), and immediately started to shiver. The wife, apparently, had a problem of changing personality. At times she would be normal and relatively happy, but much of the time she became aggressive and violent, so much so that the man was beginning to fear for the safety of his children. When touching the brooch, I immediately started to become aware of another entity, one that was obviously taking over the wife and causing her to behave in an irrational manner.

The being was a very strong and dominant female who had lived at a time when servants were considered chattles. Because of this she tried to dominate anyone with whom she came into contact in an effort to perpetuate the memory of her previous reality. The personality also seemed to be of a deeply religious and superstitious nature. With this in mind, it was possible to convince the woman to release her hold on the man's wife. She was given the option of either maintaining her power-hungry role and becoming consumed by the light, or freeing herself by releasing absolutely her hold on the physical being she was trying to control. While this was going on the room became incredibly cold, but as soon as the personality had released her hold, the room seemed to return to its normal temperature once again. Apparently the man's wife never had any more problems, even though the husband never told her of the events that had taken place.

Recently in Sydney I took part in some research into schizophrenia performed in one of the large teaching hospitals. It was research into the similarities between the brain patterns of mediums in trance and those of schizophrenics. There was a control group of 'normal' people of similar age and lifestyle, a group of schizophrenics, and a group of those people able to induce a trance — or in this case, hold an entity in their aura — at will.

What it determined was that the brain patterns of the mediums in everyday waking state were as normal as the control group; but when there was an entity being consciously held in the aura, then the brain patterns were similar to those of the schizophrenics! This research is the beginning of a search for drug-free therapy for this category of sufferers. It is believed by many psychics and healers alike that schizophrenia is but another form of spirit possession, albeit coupled with emotional or psychological symptoms, and the research, although in early stages yet, seems to back up this statement so far.

I've worked with a few schizophrenics, and invariably there is more than one entity with them, usually causing havoc, and often being responsible for the 'voices' that this particular group of people suffer from. I'm not saying that possession is the total cause behind schizophrenia, but it certainly can be responsible for many of the symptoms. Once the entities have been removed, then it is advisable for these people to receive therapy: invariably there are deep-seated emotional disturbances, and ultimately these must be dealt with before the former patients can live happy and productive lives.

In *30 Years Among the Dead* a Dr E. N. Webster of the mental health section of the American Medical Association is quoted as saying: 'I often see the spirits who cause insanity. At times I even hear their voices. Insane persons who are spoken of as hopelessly insane are frequently lost under the overwhelming control of a spirit or crowd of spirits. We frequently find by postmortem examination that no physical disorder exists in the brain or nervous system of such persons.'

Professor James Hyslop, while editor of the *Journal of the American Society for Psychical Research*, wrote: 'There is growing evidence of the fact of obsession which lies at the basis of much insanity and can be cured'. In one of his books, *Contact with the Other World*, we find the following:

The term obsession is employed by psychic researchers to denote the abnormal influence of spirits on the living...
The cures effected have required much time and patience, the use of psychotherapeutics of an unusual kind, and the employment of psychics to get into contact with the

obsessing agents and thus to release the hold which such agents have, or to educate them to voluntary abandonment of their persecutions...

As far back as 1924, Dr Wickland wrote:

Spirit obsession is a fact — a perversion of a natural law — and is amply demonstrable. This has been proven hundreds of times by causing the supposed insanity or aberration to be temporarily transferred from the victim to a psychic sensitive who is trained for the purpose, and by this method ascertain the cause of the psychosis to be an ignorant or mischievious spirit, whose identity may frequently be verified.

According to the book *Mahikari* by Dr Tebecis

...attaching spirits can interfere with, disturb or manipulate a person to varying degrees, depending on their strength, the person's attitudes, karma, power of the guardian spirit, and a number of other reasons... Disturbances by spirits may be the cause of problems ranging from minor injuries, personal discomfort, negative moods and so on to serious injuries, diseases, accidents, crime, suicide, murder and other tragedies... The disease or problem of an attaching spirit leads to the same disease or problem in the person to whom the spirit is attached.

Possession is not something that can be recognised through any particular form of learning. Rather it may be discovered through experience coupled with a strong sense of an intrusive presence, and observation of frequently irrational behaviour from the client. (It's important here to be able to tell the difference between emotional/psychological factors which determine behaviour and those produced by an entity.) It is possible for someone with clairvoyant abilities to detect an entity, maybe as a strange being, or sometimes just as negative energy, but whichever way it is recognised, it then needs to be dealt with. For once it has been discovered, it can start to give its subject an even harder time than before, to the extent of causing accidents to prevent the release from taking place.

In the book *Hostage to the Devil*, by Malachi Martin, there is a statement concerning the importance of the idea that once exorcism is engaged, it cannot be called off. According to Martin: 'Every exorcist must engage in a one-to-one confrontation, personal and bitter, with pure evil... There will and must always be a victor and a vanquished.'

The whole book deals with ritual exorcism performed according to church regulations. It shows the confrontation with evil that each exorcist must have, and the terror that the evil being can strike into the hearts of those who watch and help. It goes into explicit details of all the traumas associated with this type of evil possession, including how each case happened and how each one manifested. It fails to mention, however, any word about the light and how it can be channelled against the forces of evil. Although I've only quoted relatively harmless cases in this chapter, there have been many times when I've either faced or channelled evil in its purest sense. It is not pleasant at all, but there's another element — an external and higher power — that steps in when performing this type of healing work. To me it's channelling in its most vital role. Without that extra dimension, however, I wouldn't even contemplate challenging these entities in such a way; I wouldn't know where to start.

Some priests and their cohorts challenge such entities, and all manner of insults and negative energies are literally hurled at them. They sometimes spend days locked in confrontation with evil, and undergo the most horrific treatment. They try to banish them by force (when they can). There is no notion of the entities being souls, or any caring as to what happens to them afterwards. If the priests fail, they consider themselves at risk from then on. It is all performed with a mixture of skill (in the ritual) and terror at what might happen.

In constrast, when channelling the light there is an emphasis on the rescue aspect; the quality of this light or love energy is what determines the rescue. In this realm, it is impossible to fight force with force. As Dawn Hill says in *Edge of Reality*: 'When it comes to the use of force, you are dealing with the enemy's weapons and he is far more experienced and skilled in their use than you would ever want to be. When Christ said "Love your enemies", he was not being idealistic and philosophical; he was pointing out that love in its pure form is the only power that can defeat fear and violence'. And it does.

The other advantage of channelling is that it can be performed from a distance. A few times I've received phone calls from interstate, urgently requesting my assistance in the release of a particularly strong entity. This 'long-distance' work involves mentally 'going in search' of the being. Occasionally it's necessary to communicate with evil during the process. I'd like to quote a case that in retrospect was rather pathetic, although at the time it caused a lot of trauma.

A young boy went to the YMCA to go swimming. On his return, according to his mother, he had totally changed: he had become tearful, aggressive and extremely anti-social. Realising he had inadvertently picked up an entity, she suggested he try to get rid of 'it' himself — which he did. However, in her anxiety, she asked God that she should take it instead of him. Once the boy had released the spirit from himself, he was back to normal, but she became 'absolutely horrible', to quote her words. What had happened was that the entity had gone straight into her. Every time she breathed, her heart hurt. She was constantly moody and depressed. She wouldn't sleep with her husband, and wouldn't cook for one of her kids. Although aware enough to realise that she was behaving totally out of character and irrationally, she was unable to do anything about it.

Finally, after three weeks in this state, she became rational enough to make a long-distance telephone call, and ask for help. Due to other commitments, it was impossible for us to work on this particular issue right away. It was three days before I was able to sit down and tune in, with somebody else there to communicate with the entity.

Quite simply, it was a lost soul who had had an operation on his heart, and had believed he would survive. Not realising he could possibly be dead, he found the first available open person — the child — and took him over. Once he accepted the truth of the situation, he was happy to leave without any trouble. Within half an hour of finishing the release, the mother was on the phone. I asked her how she could tell what we had done, and she replied quite simply that suddenly she could breathe without pain, and she felt herself 'normal' again. She had waited for half an hour before calling us to make quite sure! We were separated by 3000 kilometres, but the distance had no effect at all.

As a branch of healing, soul release work is one of the quickest to take effect. It's also one of the least pleasant from my point of view, and the most dangerous to play around with. The therapist needs to know exactly what he or she is doing, and to have both experience in this realm, and the resources of the light and the beings of light who can help. A point I need to make here is that this form of psychic rescue work is not the solution to all problems. Occasionally people imagine that they are possessed, for it seems to them that they are taken over by something beyond their control. However, very often it is their own shadow side, or the result of a deep-seated trauma, that is appearing, and not an entity at all.

It is important to remember that the more evil an entity is, the less it will tolerate the light. Hence channelling the light is the most powerful method of removing these beings. For the same reason, light is used as a method of protection for many who work in this area — a protective bubble or sheath of white light is created that totally surrounds the body. Being filled with the light, or channelling this energy, is a strong spiritual insulation against psychic invasion; it has been used throughout the ages, and will continue to be used ad infinitum.

Possession can and does take place, but it is possible to release the offending entity. It is also possible to prevent it from happening in the first place, by not playing in unknown realms, and by not allowing oneself to become so dependent on drugs that the aura is no longer protective. It is important to keep one's energy as clear as possible, and this means not only on the physical level (cigarettes, alcohol and drugs all affect this energy), but also on the emotional level. It is necessary to guard against deep depression as far as possible, and when working on the spiritual level, to make sure that normal precautions are taken. The answer must be, above all, to stay true to yourself, and to allow the light to flow in your life as much as possible.

Chapter Seven

Channelling for Therapies

Throughout the world there are many therapists who, depending on their training and inclination, practise their own brand of therapy. Here I include everything from massage therapy and bodywork to psychotherapy and past life therapy. All come under the umbrella of 'therapy', with many professionals working in a variety of fields, synthesising their multi-faceted knowledge.

Over the years I've noticed a distinct difference between the therapists I would classify as adequate, and the special ones who seem to have that extra, indefinable 'something' which often gives them a certain charisma. I believe that this quality is an extension of the other senses — a tuning in on a higher level than is considered usual. Such therapists appear highly intuitive, and are able to work in a deeper and more fulfilling way with their clients. Many of these therapists are what I would term 'naturals', often having no concept of their extra sensitivity. If asked, they would probably put their success down to expertise in their particular field — of course that is important too, but it's not what I'm referring to here. I've watched certain therapists with qualifications and lists of initials after their name, whom I wouldn't send my worst enemy to. Yet the converse is also true: I've watched people with few official qualifications do amazing work with their clients. As a general rule, it is safer to find someone who has knowledge as well as skills. However, the ones who are highly recommended are usually those who fit into the category of being special in some way.

I've spent many years working with a wide variety of therapists, healers and teachers, and those that have left an impression have always had that added quality. What it comes down to is an ability to 'shift gears' out of the formal, learned methods into whatever 'feels' right at the time. As one therapist put it: 'I have a lot of fancy cars in my garage, but I don't need them any more'. In other words he no longer relies on learned techniques and processes, but on his 'gut feeling' — with amazing results.

With those whose work I have studied, I have observed a subtle change at certain times during therapy sessions or workshops. It's as if the person very gently flows into another energy, or allows another energy to flow into and through him/her. It is a very gentle transference into channelling without any perceptible change, and is only noticeable if you are really aware of energies or if you are one of those people able (clairvoyantly) to see energies or energy beings.

I remember watching Elisabeth Kübler-Ross, the world famous authority on death and dying, many years ago. I listened to her lecture, and during the talk it appeared to me as if she, as a person, almost disappeared, and in her place was another, far larger and more masculine being. In fact when I commented on it to her at a later date, she just smiled enigmatically!

When I watched her working in a workshop, it was even more fascinating. When she tuned into someone and was totally in harmony with them, the channelling taking place was almost visible on a physical level. As soon as her work was over, and the person had gone back to his or her place in the group, she reverted to being her normal self. It was totally spontaneous, and happened off and on throughout the course of the workshop. The deeper the piece of work with the client, the more likely it was to happen.

Over the years I've had many comments from people who have watched me lecture or run workshops, and I know that often I'm not totally there, but that another energy is coming in. One person commented that I seemed to totally disappear on one occasion, and described what seemed to be there in my place. It was fascinating — even more so when I realise that I can't remember a thing that I said in that particular lecture!

In the book *Opening to Channel*, one of the co-authors, Duane Packer, comments on how he sees the change take place:

When I observe people channelling, I see a real difference in their energy fields as they shift out of what they call their 'intuitive' selves — which I see as a harmonizing and smoothing of their energies — and into the guides' space,

pulling information and a boost of energy from somewhere outside of themselves. When I talk to people and
point out to them when I see the shift, they can almost
always identify a change at the same time in their physical
sensations, in their thoughts, or in the messages they are
receiving.

Much of this book consists of information channelled from
the guides of the two authors. One of these guides talks about
Duane's development in therapy work: 'Duane learned many of
the standard bodywork techniques and frameworks of thought.
He did his energy work using those frameworks until a new one
began to emerge that went beyond them. As Duane began to see
'density patterns' around the body, he realised that he was seeing
the physical energy fields, the emotional body and the mental
body. When all were harmonised, the spiritual shimmer became
visible.'

When Duane first began to 'see', he was working by day as a
scientist with a PhD in geology/geophysics, and by night as a
bodyworker, teaching and healing. He had methodically
researched every bodywork technique he could find — from
Eastern approaches such as acupressure and related disciplines
to Western approaches; deep tissue massage therapy, kinesiol-
ogy, and so on. At one stage of his development, he gave up his
'seeing' abilities because he was scared for his sanity. However, in
time he came back to it, and started to learn more and to
understand clearly what was happening.

He began to 'see' into the muscles and physical structure,
'knowing' where to touch and what to do to end certain kinds of
pain, release past-life or current-life trauma, and repattern the
energy bodies (the physical, emotional and mental) into their
higher spiritual pattern. He began to see telepathic cords from
others in people's body and energy fields, and found he could
take them out, creating almost instantaneous changes in
people's lives. By starting with a framework that he could learn
and operate from, he eventually evolved through and beyond it
into his and DaBen's (his guide's) own methods.

Several bodywork students who were also channels have been
able, through their work with Duane and DaBen and their own

guides, to see the same energy patterns and create many similar results.

I have a close friend and colleague who works in a similar way. When she first started working in this field she used to be quite apprehensive about all she could see and sense. Now, with experience behind her, she is able to utilise the skills to bring about changes in people's lives — whether on an emotional or physical level. Using what she sees, she will trigger the person, either through touch or appropriate words, into releasing whatever is necessary. As she progresses in a session there is the previously mentioned sense of her physical presence diminishing as another energy comes through. Once there, the clarity with which she functions is amazing.

Sometimes during a session I have the experience of saying words that I had absolutely no concept of before I started to speak. It's as if the words almost say themselves and I'm only the intermediary for them, to see that they reach their destination. Invariably these words that come without prior knowledge are very powerful in one sense or another. They might touch a deep chord in the person, or trigger some type of energy release — whatever seems necessary at the time. What also happens is that the same words keep repeating themselves in my mind, especially if I'm being particularly obtuse, and nothing else will come until I have spoken them. After that it's as if a whole stream has been released, and the words just keep flowing until there are no more.

This process is explained by Orin (guide to Sanaya Roman, the other co-author of *Opening to Channel*) and DaBen at a later stage in the book:

> To trigger your voice, we normally use your thoughts. When you are channelling, we are the undercurrent beneath your thoughts, the part that selects which thoughts to trigger, that causes your mind to speak of certain things, in a particular way. We light up certain areas of your mind, and we also trigger your own soul's knowledge. We draw not our ideas, but the words necessary to express them from your mind. The richer your mind is with knowledge and experience, the more words we have to choose from to express our thought-impulses.

Sometimes I work with people who have done years of personal growth work, but there's still that elusive something that seems to be missing. Allie was one such person: since adolescence she had suffered from a stomach ulcer. This not only gave her recurrent pain and discomfort, but meant that she had to be extremely careful of what she ate — not an easy task for an airline stewardess. However, the final piece of the jigsaw continued to elude her.

By the time she came to me as a client, she had spent years working through meditation techniques, rebirthing, EST-type courses, psychotherapy, spiritual healing, and a whole host of more conventional therapies, medically prescribed drugs and a wide variety of diets. She felt she was close to the end of her struggle, but was aware that she needed outside energy to find 'the last piece of the jigsaw'.

In fact, there were two pieces of the jigsaw left to be fitted together, and they both fell into place in the one session I did with her. Having tuned in to Allie on a relatively deep level, I became aware of some huge shock that she had sustained as a tiny, newborn infant. However, as I became aware of this, it had to take second place, as the energy being generated triggered her spontaneously into a past-life experience that was necessary to release first.

She had been a child in Holland approximately 100 years ago. She had lived in a poverty-stricken household with a mentally retarded and dumb father, and a mother who had to do all the work. One day the father walked out of the house and drowned himself. The mother did nothing to restrain him and, presumably due to guilt, went crazy. In one of her fits she started attacking the child with a kitchen knife, but stumbled over a table leg. As she fell to the ground, she hit her head on the table and dropped the knife. The child immediately grabbed it, and still in terror, drove the knife into her mother's stomach, killing her.

Horrified by what she had done, the child stayed alone in the house and finally starved to death, filled with a mixture of terror and guilt. Once the death had been experienced, I took the spirit of the child — the spirit of Allie now — through a process of forgiving both her mother and herself. Then we went through a process of integration before finally coming back into this life, not in the present, but at the time of 'suffering a severe shock as a tiny baby'.

She immediately became aware of herself as a tiny baby who had just been born, and whose umbilical cord was being cut. This action triggered the subconscious memory of the guilt and pain from the previous life. The shock was so great that she seemed to leave her body for three days, acting as if frozen within the pain. When I checked up with her later I discovered that during the first three days of her life she hadn't moved, hadn't cried and had refused to eat.

Once we had released the pain of the past, Allie was able to come back to the present day. In her mind, I gave her the baby that had been her, to love and hold. Afterwards, she was able to take part in her own healing process by allowing the light energy to flow into all parts of her body, giving special attention to her solar plexus and abdomen. At the same time I gave her healing and balanced her energy centres.

For much of this process there was a part of me functioning on what I term 'overdrive' — the part which I no longer controlled and which was being used by a higher energy to achieve some healing and therapeutic process. When this happens it's as if the words come out of my mouth before I have time to conceptualise them, and there's a deep 'knowingness' as to what has to be done, and a sense of being part of a greater flow.

I monitored Allie fairly closely over the next few days, and daily she was aware of physical improvements. When I heard from her recently, she had continued with her healing process and had had no pain or gastric trouble for many months now.

One of the major lessons I have learnt from this type of therapy concerns trust — trust in the process itself, as well as trust in whatever is behind the energy and awareness which I am given. There have been many times when my logical mind has shrieked for help. Almost as if it were daring that external 'something' to solve the problem.

On two separate occasions the solution needed concerned the death experience. The first time was when someone physically 'died' while re-living the death experience in a past life. As I became aware of the reality of the situation, I also became aware of an enormous flow of energy coming through me and into my patient. At the same time my voice changed and became more forceful and powerful. The patient started rebreathing, somewhat annoyed that he had been 'dragged back from such a beautiful space'.

The next time was amusing in retrospect, but all I could think at the time was: 'What on earth can I tell her husband?'. Again, it was after the death experience in a past life, but this time she didn't physically 'die'. She just made a very determined decision that it was so peaceful and beautiful after the hell she had been through, that she wasn't going to come back. My immediate reaction was: 'God, give me inspiration'. Certainly I started talking before I had any idea of what to say. In essence what I said was: 'If you choose to go now, you will have to relive in entirety the whole of your current life next time round'. As her life had been both difficult and painful for many years, I knew the power of those words. She came back immediately!

After both these experiences I realised how much I relied on forces beyond myself, and how important it is for me to understand the potential of channelling in this context. There is no doubt in my mind that I would frequently be in very uncomfortable territory if I didn't work with this added energy. I often say a heartfelt 'thank you' at the end of a particularly tricky session, especially when I truly don't have an understanding of how we ended up where we did. Even more common are the times when I go into a session on one tack, and end up in a totally different place, and yet both are absolutely necessary to the process. I'll explain what I mean.

Peter came to me with a crippling back injury that had forced him to give up the work he loved, breeding and training horses. He lived, albeit reluctantly, on medical compensation. In his X-ray, two ruptured intervertebral discs showed up. The surgeon wanted to operate in order to minimise the pain he was suffering, and as Peter could think of no other solution, a date was set.

In the interim he happened to arrive at the healing centre my husband and I were running. Ostensibly there on holiday, it soon became apparent there were other reasons for him being there. The interesting point here is that Peter never complained about his back. He was so resigned about it, and the forthcoming operation, that it faded into insignificance amongst everything else that was happening. One day someone had an accident, and I suggested that Peter give her some healing. His reaction was quite startling. He visibly blanched, looked really shaken, and then told me he couldn't.

As I was aware of a really strong healing energy within him, I asked him what was going on. As a result we ended up in a session aimed at clearing this block about healing. I consciously took him back to a time when he had been a travelling healer, prior to the time of Christ. He had started off with good intentions, but gradually the power had gone to his head, and he started to boast of his own prowess. Eventually the local priests caught up with him and threatened him with crucifixion — the common method of disposing of criminals in those days — unless he acknowledged where his power came from.

Being so enmeshed in his ego, he was unable to change his outlook. He also believed that he had the power to escape whatever punishment was given him. However, this was not the case, and he suffered incredible pain once he was strung up on the cross — so much so that eventually he was forced to acknowledge his own weakness, publically, and they cut him down and left him. He crawled away, his back dislocated beyond repair, and eventually died in pain and shame from the experience.

The next step was for him to forgive his killers, which was easy, and then to forgive himself for his misguided ego. The latter was far harder and took quite some time. Eventually he was able to let go of all that had happened, and come forward into the present day without the guilt, shame and belief systems that he had been carrying for so long. Two aspects here had led to his present trouble: one was that any back injury led to becoming a total cripple in his eyes. The other was that being a healer or giving healing ultimately led to death. When one memory was triggered, even at the subconscious level, the other would automatically be triggered.

Over the two weeks following this session, Peter was subjected to all types of physical stress. This included lifting huge lengths of timber, building, and working extremely long hours under harsh conditions. Not only did his back not trouble him, but he seemed to thrive on the work. After this, he returned to his orthopaedic surgeon. Another X-ray was taken, and the surgeon was stunned. There was nothing wrong with the discs; Peter could touch his toes and perform all the designated tests, pain-free. The surgeon spent the next hour listening to what had happened.

Peter now works part-time as a very successful healer, and runs his own courses in healing. As a channel, he also works with people in terms of their past lives or their current life, whichever is necessary. He no longer makes the mistake of believing that his healing is all his own power.

What I need to emphasise here is how the channelling takes us to dimensions of which we were often not previously aware. Peter was taken back nearly 2000 years to release an intense physical problem as well as a deep-seated emotional block.

Sometimes it is the energy itself that catapults the person back to the relevant incident. I had been lecturing in an Australian city, and afterwards one woman was particularly insistent that I work with her. When I took her hand to tune in, it was as if the energy set off a time bomb. She just screamed and screamed and screamed for some minutes (she had never done any previous growth work) and then worked through a really powerful session. Obviously the channelling had triggered the crux of her problem, and with very little work on my part, she had released whatever was necessary.

This set me to realising not only how powerful this type of work can be, but also how potentially dangerous it can be in the hands of the inexperienced. People often get carried away with channelling when they first start to use it, and feel that because they *are* channelling, it must be safe. Maybe this is so for some, but when you are dealing with people's minds, with their sanity in fact, you can never be too careful. In the past I've frequently had calls from people — many complete strangers — who have had bad experiences in groups or even during individual therapy, and feel a part of them is still trapped in the past. Whether it's in a past life, or more rarely, in early childhood, is immaterial. There is a strange sense of not being quite within the body, of being disconnected from reality, and a difficulty in focusing. For those of you who have astral travelled and then not properly returned, it's akin to that.

Many people use hypnosis for regression work with remarkable success. However, there are times when there are adverse effects here too, usually as a result of the therapist's inexperience or lack of understanding. One client came to me because, although she was walking around in the twentieth century, her mind was still half in the nineteenth century. Looking at her was like seeing double: it was as if her energy/spirit body wasn't properly in her physical body.

What had happened was that she had gone into a past life, but then hadn't come out of it properly. She not only hadn't resolved the relevant issue, but she had been brought back too quickly to the present day, and part of her consciousness was still trapped in the past.

It wasn't hard, using the stimulus of channelled energy and the awareness of the regression process, to take her completely back to the previous life, resolve the issue, and then bring all of her forwards into the 'now'. She was a far happier and more comfortable person by the end of the session.

I believe there is a very real place for awareness on other levels as well as the use of channelling in the various therapies available. It means the therapist has a greater range of possibilities at his/her command, and can follow the client into the areas not written about in normal text books. It may not be as cut and dried as therapy on the purely physical level, but it gives the client more freedom to explore all levels — the physical, emotional and spiritual — and to find the wholeness within.

Chapter Eight

The Light — and How to Use It

In this chapter I intend to cover some of the preparatory exercises necessary for getting in contact with one's inner guidance, and how to prepare to channel in a safe and loving way. There are many different ways to reach the same end, and what appears here will be but a sample of what is both possible and appropriate.

Maybe the simplest way to start is through understanding the term, 'the light'. This is a way of describing the energy that comes through from a higher consciousness; the higher the source of this consciousness, the brighter will be the sense of light. On many occasions when I've been working with someone, towards the end of a session I've opened my eyes to check out the sunlight that is suddenly flooding the room. Without fail, there is no difference in the sun — it can even be pouring with rain outside — the light is on an inner level. Some people are aware of it with their eyes open, but most find it easier to sense with their eyes closed.

The light is an energy source that is almost impossible to describe. It is similar to intense sunlight, almost blinding, but always accompanied by a deep feeling of peace and love, sometimes overwhelming in its intensity. To me it's a reflection of total love and power in the highest spiritual sense, and in its presence I know that nothing is impossible. Hence when I am healing, especially when I'm working in the less pleasant aspects, I can have total trust in the power of the light.

The very basic preliminary exercises I teach people before even tuning in to the light, are those of cleansing and protection. Cleansing is to shake off unwanted negativity from the aura or energy field surrounding the body. We are like sponges in that we collect energy from the atmosphere around us. If we walk into an overcrowded shopping centre, full of frenetic energy from the countless shoppers, then the chances are considerable that we will pick up some of that energy. We may start feeling tired, depressed, angry and so on. It can be quite simple to shake off these unwanted vibrations, although it's more sensible to prevent them accumulating in the first place. What follows is a physical method of cleansing the energy body.

Cleansing
Find a comfortable position, and place your hands with the palms facing towards your face, about 1 centimetre from your brow, and parallel with it. With gentle, sweeping movements, move your hands along the forehead, and flick off the energy as if flicking off water. Starting in the same position again, move the hands up and over the head, down to the nape of the neck and across the shoulders, again flicking off the unwanted energy. Do this three or four times in both positions, and you may find yourself experiencing a shivering sensation up and down your spine.

This shiver is a sign that you are cleansed, but you do not have to experience it to feel cleansed. While some people will feel it, others have different methods of knowing: some may feel more alive or alert, with others it's just a 'knowingness', and still others may take a time before they are aware of any sensation following the experience. It is something I still do regularly between clients, so that I don't carry the energy from the previous one into the next session. However, in time, it's possible to think in terms of being cleansed or having the intention of being cleansed, and this is sufficient for it to take place; or to imagine standing under a waterfall, with the water cleansing the whole energy system. In workshops I teach people the basic method, then after a couple of days get them to tune in to their own inner guidance and find the most suitable and appropriate method for themselves.

As well as cleansing, it is advisable to perform some technique for protecting the energy field. Each physical body has five subtle energy bodies surrounding it: the innermost one (pre-physical) being the etheric body, and the outer one (at full arm's stretch) being the spiritual body. However, it's the astral or emotional body (a few centimetres out from the physical) that is the most susceptible to external vibrations or negative energy.

This is the one that is the most important to protect, especially in the early stages of meditation and healing.

Protection
The simplest method of protection, and one that can be used at any time and in any place, is that of creating a bubble of white light, a cocoon of protection, around your whole being. Simply imagine a bubble of light totally surrounding your whole body, paying special attention to the area under the feet, the back of the head, and the spine — especially the back of the heart centre — and if you wish, you can seal it with a cross, or any symbol that is pertinent to you and your philosophy. If you have problems visualising, don't worry. It's quite possible to do this adequately through intention alone, or just feeling the sensation of the bubble. Another simple method of protection which some of you may prefer is to imagine a dot of light right in the centre of your being. Allow this dot to grow and grow until it totally surrounds you in a protective sheath, and feel the strength of this light sheath.

There is also a method which incorporates cleansing and protection: using a white light meditation. This is a method of drawing the universal energy into your whole body in such a way that it cleanses, revitalises, recharges and protects you, and leaves you with a general feeling of well-being and peace.

White light meditation
Find a comfortable position where it is possible to relax without any interruptions. (Take the phone off the hook, put a sign on the door and so on.) Close your eyes and very gently start to breathe in a slow and regular rhythm, inhaling first from the base of your stomach, followed by your diaphragm and finally your chest; then exhaling from your chest, your diaphragm, and finally from your stomach. Allow this pattern of breathing to relax you, and at the same time, imagine all the tension that it stored in your body being breathed out with every exhalation. Gradually let the breathing become even and regular, until it forms a natural part of your meditation.

When you are comfortable with this breathing technique, then imagine an infinite light source (such as the sun) just above your head, pouring down white light. Imagine/visualise/feel this light like a waterfall that is very gently flowing down through your body, cleansing and healing you . . . Feel it flowing through your head, your throat and neck, and into your heart centre where is situated the bud of a flower. As the light flows into this heart-centre flower, the bud very gently starts to open, and the more it opens, the more the light flows into it . . . Finally the flower is wide open, and the light is pouring into it and overflowing down into the solar plexus area, where it irradiates every part of that centre, and then continues downwards into the sacral centre (the centre in the pelvis) into the root (the centre at the base of the spine), and then down the legs, through the feet, and out into the earth below.

Once the light is flowing through the whole of your body, then allow it to expand outwards while it is still flowing downwards. This light is now your protection as well as your cleansing; feel it permeating every atom of your being, and enjoy it. Feel the power of the light, and know that while you are in the light and surrounded by the light, nothing negative can get near you. See this light as a reflective shield: as much love energy as you wish can flow both in and out, but anything negative coming towards you gets repelled by the shield's surface . . .

Bring the awareness of how it feels back to your physical presence. Now concentrate your awareness on each part of your body in turn, making sure you can feel the aliveness coming back into the physical, then very gently you can return to the present, and open your eyes. Stay where you are for a few minutes, and don't move in a hurry for you could find yourself a little spaced out. Make sure your feet are flat on the floor, to ground yourself, and breathe gently, giving yourself time to adjust to being back in reality.

This is a very simple yet amazingly powerful meditation, and if practised regularly, can have profound effects. These effects can include not only heightened spiritual awareness, but an enhanced feeling of well-being, and may also lead to cleansing on an inner level. This cleansing could be in a physical form, such as a cold or a brief stomach upset which would be releasing toxins from the body; or it might be on an emotional level, such as increased sensitivity to people and events or releasing suppressed emotions, maybe through crying.

Don't be afraid of any of these for they are all Nature's way of healing. If emotions are allowed to build up and up, your body becomes like a pressure cooker, until finally it can take no more and it has to explode. This explosion may be in the form of an illness or disease, or it may be through releasing tears or anger. Whatever the method of release, the end result will be change for the positive, so keep on with the meditation. Regular practice is what counts, preferably daily, and at the same time if possible. You may start to feel positive results straight away, but even if you don't, do persevere for a while and give yourself a chance.

The next step in going within is to create a special place in your mind where you can actually meet with and communicate with your higher self, your guide, your God part, or your superconsciousness — whatever you choose to call it.

Creating your sanctuary (or meeting a wise being) meditation
Find a relaxed position where you will be free of any interruptions, and very gently start the breathing technique described in the previous section. As you feel the tension draining out of your body, imagine yourself in a place in nature that is special to you. It may be a wood, a garden, a deserted beach, anywhere that is alive and has a special feeling for you . . . Once you have imagined yourself in this place, then let yourself both see and feel everything that is there: feel the ground — is it hard or soft, is it earth or sand or grass? How does it smell; how does it feel to be there? What else is there with you? Can you hear or see the birds, the insects; can you feel their vitality as they go about their daily routine? What about flowers, plants, trees — can you sense their presence, see them, touch them, feel their energy, their colour, their life? Allow yourself to draw in energy from all that is around you; feel it filling up your being, and be aware of *how* it feels . . .

(If you have any difficulty in doing this exercise, then it's advisable only to go this far for the moment. Practise it daily until if feels really comfortable for you. Don't have a preconditioned idea that you *must* be able to see clearly; it may be that you work best through your feelings, and so clear vision isn't a part of your make-up at this time. Don't worry, just appreciate what you *can* do, and know that in time and with practice, everything becomes easier.)

Once you are comfortable in your special place in nature, then you can continue: become aware of the sun beating gently down on you with a comfortable warmth, and as you feel its presence, become aware also of a light fall of rain — a sun-shower. As a result of this sun-shower, a beautiful rainbow appears, but it's a rainbow with a difference. This rainbow never moves, but acts like a bridge for you to travel through to another dimension . . . Feel youself being drawn towards this rainbow, maybe to one particular colour, and very gently allow yourself to move up this rainbow until you find yourself in a mountain pasture. Feel the grass beneath your feet, the tiny flowers spread all around, and become aware of mountains in the distance . . .

Not far away is a special place that draws you gently towards it. This place is your sanctuary or temple; a place where you can go for healing, for guidance, for peace, or for whatever you need or choose . . . As you get closer to this sanctuary or temple, become aware of how it looks, how it feels to you, and what it's made of. Become aware now of the entrance to your sanctuary, and there waiting for you is a wise being, a special person who is there only for you. Feel the being's presence, and feel the loving energy that is radiating from him or her toward you. Let this energy into your being . . .

Now follow your wise being inside your sanctuary, and let yourself be led towards the heart of your sanctuary. This is your place of healing. Open yourself to the energy that is here, and feel it entering into your being . . . Allow yourself to remain in this energy for a while, and then when you are ready, open your mind to your wise being, and ask whatever you wish to know. The understanding may come as words, it may come as thoughts or just as a 'knowingness'. However it comes, be open to it, and allow it to be . . . When you feel you have received as much as you are able to absorb for the moment, thank your being, and start to make your way back to the entrance to your sanctuary.

Once you are at the entrance, you may take your leave of your wise being, knowing that you can come back whenever you

choose . . . Move toward the rainbow that you came up on and
feel yourself flowing down the rainbow, back to your favourite
place in nature, and very gently start becoming aware of your
body. Feel the muscles, the joints, the limbs, and allow the
energy to flow freely within your body . . . When you are totally
aware of yourself as a physical being, then bring your
consciousness back into the room in which you are sitting or
lying, and in your own time, open your eyes and come back to
reality.

Again, don't move too quickly, but allow yourself some space
in which you can just be with what has taken place.

After you get used to this particular type of meditation, you
can extend what you do in your sanctuary. For example, you can
create a garden for yourself — fill it with all the flowers, trees,
plants and animals you can think of; be as creative as you like.
Or you can bathe in a cleansing pool — really enjoy the
immersion, and how it feels to be totally cleansed by this water;
some people find they are joined here by dolphins or other water
creatures. Or you might like to explore rooms of colour and feel
each colour in turn. Only your mind limits what you can do in
this dimension, so enjoy the exploration. Remember also that
here, any questions can be answered; if you have a problem that
is too much for you to handle, here you can hand it over to a
higher being or presence and ask for help with the solution. As
you become more accustomed to tuning in to your higher being
on this level, so too will you find it easier on a day-to-day level.

According to *The Course in Miracles*: 'The only requirement
for hearing your inner guide is your willingness'. However,
many people also suffer from confusion, especially in the early
stages, which is why I suggest doing the meditation to gain
easier access in the beginning. To contact one's inner guidance
— 'the still, small voice' within — it is necessary to be still. You
need to let go of all thoughts, desires, ideas, and to still your
mind — not an easy task when we have been brought up to be
busy doing or thinking something all the time. It is also
important to trust what comes through and not to have an
investment in a particular answer. In other words, to accept that
your inner guide truly knows what's best for you, even if you
don't understand it at the time.

However — and this is very important — if you feel uncomfortable with what you are hearing, then maybe you are not in a sufficiently still space, or perhaps your hearing has become confused, and it would be most unwise to follow any messages in this fashion. Only go with what you feel good about. There is a difference between not understanding and not feeling good about something. If it resonates to you at a gut level, then you know it is right. You also need to learn to accept the answer that comes, even if it's not what you were expecting, for often our wants are not in accordance with what's best for us. If any feelings of doubt creep in, then just keep listening. Once the real answer is there, you will feel the peace, the certainty: you will know.

In his book *Listening*, Lee Coit states that: 'God's voice is everywhere. Since all things are echoes of God's Voice, be open to all sources. The truth will stay and the rest will pass by. Songs, books, ideas, friends, and even enemies all speak for God's love, so set aside time each day to listen and to write. Willingness is the only condition for listening'.

Guided writing
Once tuned in, many people find that words start flowing when they are holding a writing implement over a piece of paper, almost as if that small act makes the connection. Start asking very simple questions in the early stages such as: 'Am I properly cleansed and protected', or 'What colour would it be most helpful for me to wear today', and as your confidence builds up, then you can ask questions that you really need answers to, including those of an esoteric nature. Try not to rationalise what comes through. At first you may feel that it's your own ego talking, but once you start getting answers to questions you had no idea about, then your confidence will start to build. It's important that you remember to cleanse and protect before attempting this, every time, then centre yourself, find your peace within, and tune in.

Some people find that an easy exercise is to tune in under the shower each day and mentally ask for a word for the day from within. This usually comes without much trouble, and may be a reflection on the day; it may be a word to help you cope with what is going to happen, or it may capture the whole quality of the day ahead. When this comes easily, start to ask for information on a wider scale that will help you throughout the next 24 hours. If you don't understand something, or it is not crystal clear for you, then ask for clarity. Don't put up with second best when the best is possible: you need to understand what you are receiving, and confused messages are just not acceptable.

If you have no tried method of becoming centred, then it's worth looking at a method taught by Thomas Crum. A teacher of conflict resolution through the art of Aiki, Crum's work is based on the philosophy of aikido, a Japanese martial art. In his book *The Magic of Conflict*, he mixes both the theory and practice of aikido with anecdotes and exercises that help the reader resolve the conflicts of everyday life. To him, life is a playground wherein conflict can be resolved naturally and peacefully, bringing us closer in touch with our true self: a fully integrated mind, body and spirit.

In *The Magic of Conflict*, Thomas Crum writes:

The first condition of the Aiki Approach is: CHOOSE TO BE CENTRED . . . Centering is a real psychophysiological experience that each of us can choose to have, right now.

We have all experienced centering. It occurs when the mind, body and spirit become fully integrated in dynamic balance and connectedness with the world around us. There is a heightened awareness and sensitivity, a feeling that everything is perfect the way it is. The truth of who we are as human beings is revealed. The centred state is simple, natural, and powerful. Understanding centre is useful only if we truly integrate it into our mind and body and use it.

The centre of gravity of an object has been defined as: 'an infinitely small point upon which an entire object can be balanced' — in other words, a dynamically active, vibrationally alive centre of balance and stability.

One of the simplest exercises demonstrated by Thomas Crum during his teaching session illustrates the power of centering. Using someone from the audience, he has the person stand beside him and very lightly he places the finger tips of one hand above the centre of the person's chest. Slowly he increases the pressure while the person physically resists. With very little pressure the person starts to wobble. He then repeats the same exercise while having the person concentrate on his/her own centre — in standing this is roughly 2 inches below the navel — and to help with the concentration, he gets them to touch their centre during the exercise. Then he increases the pressure again, but this time, there is much more stability, and the pressure can be increased considerably more than the first time. All this is achieved through the person's simple awareness of his or her natural centre.

The following centering exercise recommended by Thomas Crum is a simple one; it is similar to a meditative technique.

Centering

Starting as before with deep and even breathing, imagine the tension flowing our of your body . . . Imagine now a beam of light extending from your centre out through the the top of your head, picturing your centre as about the size of a large ball. Allow the light beam to swing from side to side, taking your whole upper body with it, and maintain this swinging motion for a few moments to establish the natural rhythm. Continue the swing, letting the centre become smaller and smaller by half its size each time until there's no more body movement. Even if your centre becomes so small you can no longer visualise it, still focus on the vibration of your centre as it diminishes to infinity.

The focusing of attention on an ever-decreasing point allows for 'a comfortable ride inward to the source of your being'. If thoughts come into your mind, just bring your attention back to the vibratory quality of your centre. This quality may be perceived differently by each individual, but just become aware of how you perceive it, allowing it to take whatever form it chooses. This process should be practised for 15 to 20 minutes daily, again ending slowly and gently as in the previous techniques.

This centering technique is almost a meditation in itself, and no book on channelling can be complete without mentioning the importance of meditation in day-to-day living, let alone its importance in contacting one's inner guidance. If I asked ten different people what they believed meditation to be, their answers would most likely vary considerably. To me, meditation is a very powerful technique of letting go, going within, and getting in touch with the source. To you it may be as simple as relaxation after a heavy day's work; to others it may be a technique for accessing what lies hidden beneath the surface of normal, waking consciousness. To White Eagle, the spirit channelled by Grace Cooke, 'Meditation is the true way to unfold the spiritual awareness of truth which arises from the heart. It is really the awakening of the heart centre, by love'.

As there are many ideas as to what meditation is (and isn't), so too are there many methods, and the art is to find the one or ones that suit you the best. Some poeple use a *mantra* — a repeated word or words from the Sanskrit language which have a vibratory sound. These sounds are said to represent various aspects of God. In Western civilisation, many people are now using *mantras* from their own language, either chosen by themselves, or given to them by a teacher. Some techniques teach you to focus on your breathing or on your heartbeat or on music, while others use a thought or quality to focus on, such as love or the energy of the Christ Consciousness. Mandalas or special pictures can be used as a focus, as can a candle flame; some people do what is termed an active or dynamic meditation using movement as the focusing agent. Whatever the method, the desire is the same throughout — to go within, to hear 'the still, small voice', to access the subconscious, to connect with one's inner being.

For anyone wanting to connect with his/her source within, meditation is one of the best ways of doing so. It is an invaluable tool that, practised daily, can bring about many positive changes. I cannot stress too highly the value of both the action and the discipline of meditating if you truly want to live a more productive, creative and fulfilling life.

Meditation is the listening part of prayer. It is in the stillness that we hear clearest our inner messages, whether from the God source, our Higher Self, or guides. But how do we know for sure that what we are hearing is for real? Although I have mentioned this before, I need also to bring it into the context of this chapter.

It is up to you to discriminate. Do not blindly accept everything you hear from an inner voice or from a discarnate spirit using someone else's voice. You do not automatically accept whatever you hear in everyday life, so why should it be any different in this context? In time, you will learn to recognise and trust everything you receive, *knowing* that its source is pure, and what is being said is valid. While you are learning however, it's advisable only to accept those messages that feel right, that strike a chord in the deepset aspects of your being. Pure guidance will assist you in your life; it will be for the highest good and will not be frightening, or have negative motives or associations.

Use your commonsense: something that is good will not leave you feeling powerless or scared or uncomfortable. Your guidance or guides speak with love and compassion — you can feel it; you feel good with it. Your guidance may advise, but will never dictate. Be aware if ever you are told you MUST do something — know that all is not well, and double check:

— Did you cleanse and protect?
— Were you centred?
— Did you go into the silence with love, or were you still in an emotional or confused state?

Keep these questions as a check list just in case, but as always, prevention is better than cure. Remember the preliminaries, and have a clear intention of what you want to achieve. Remember also that some people will never actually hear their communication: it might come in the form of pictures, feelings, a 'knowingness', symbols or even colours. Whatever happens for you, allow yourself to accept, rather than trying to manipulate and change things to the way you want them. We all perceive things in our own unique way, and no one way is better than another any more than one person is better than another: we just *are*.

As I write this there are words repeating in my consciousness: 'Open your heart to the light and all will be very, very well. Doubt not in your own ability, for you have the power to receive as you have the power to give, and as you trust in your own process, the knowledge and wisdom will flow and you will become one with the God force within you'.

As this isn't a 'how to' book, I'm not going to spend time on teaching how to channel per se. This is something that I feel needs a lot of preparation and is best learnt directly from someone with knowledge and experience as well as an open heart, not from a book. There can be no substitute for the human contact, and this way is not only far safer, but you have the support and encouragement necessary. However, it is useful to have a working knowledge of healing so that you can practise channelling healing energy for yourself, your family and friends.

I will reiterate that the clearer you are of your own emotional rubbish, then the clearer a channel you become. This works both for tuning in to your own inner guidance, and also for channelling energy for healing and so on. Apart from practising the exercises described earlier in this chapter, it's as well to give yourself the opportunity to release any deep-seated blocks that might be holding you back. Whether you do this through meditation, therapy, silent retreat, workshops, or healing is totally your choice. What is important is that it is right for you, and you feel good with the results — it doesn't matter how you achieve these results.

The most important point to remember when healing is compassion or caring. If that quality is not there, then it doesn't matter what you do; you will not achieve the results you want. If you are healing purely for your ego to receive a boost such as 'Aren't you clever', or 'What a good healer you are', then think again. This attitude will only lead you into trouble. True healing comes through the heart — the centre of unconditional love. In the heart centre, the universal energy (whether it is the God force, from guides, or from the collective unconscious) and the earth energy meet and are transformed into the healing power of unconditional love.

When you are ready to heal, you will find it isn't a big issue. It is something totally natural if you can just let it flow; however I will give you a few pointers to help you get started. From then on it is up to you and your inner guidance. I'm a firm believer in letting each individual tune in to the person being healed so that

they do what feels right and appropriate for them at the time.
There is no set way to be followed; just allow the energy to flow
to direct you.

Preparation for healing

Before you start, remember the preliminaries: cleanse and
protect first, then protect yourself and your patient together in
what I term a double bubble, then check you are centred. Next
you tune in to the higher energy, mentally asking that healing
energy should flow through you and into the person needing
healing, for the highest good of all. Once at this stage, stop a
moment, and feel your grounding. Can you feel the earth's
natural energy flowing up into you? Can you feel where it meets
with the higher energy in your heart centre? Now imagine the
flower in your heart centre gently opening.

Tuning in

Tune in to the energy of the other person in whatever way feels
most comfortable to you. If you are healing with the person
sitting on a stool or chair in front of you, then the easiest way to
tune in is to put your hands lightly on his or her shoulders and
keep them there for a while or until you have felt what needs to
happen next. You can also, very carefully, tune in to the energy
above the crown centre, keeping your hands a few inches above
the person's head. This is a very sensitive area, and some people
cannot handle anyone working on them here, while for others
there is no problem at all. Feel your patient out, and endeavour
to remain flexible. From both these positions it is possible to
become aware of all that is happening for the other person: the
location of problems such as pain and discomfort. You may feel
a sense of where to go from here, such as a strong inner nudging
to work on the heart centre or throat. Follow your feeling. In the
beginning you may be unsure, but with practice, the clarity will
increase, and so too will your trust in the whole process.

If your patient is lying face down, you can tune in by putting
one hand gently over the root centre at the base of the spine. Feel
on an energy level first — coming down gently until approximately 2 cm away from the body — before you actually touch
the physical, and there let it rest. Very sensitively, feel with your

other hand up the spine, slowly moving it up to the head and back again so that you get the opportunity to really feel the energy between your hand and the person's back. You'll find this will become easier with practice. Be aware of temperature differences and any other sensations that may be apparent.

Healing

If you simply have a friend with a headache, then follow all the preliminary steps, holding your hands in the most appropriate place for the energy to channel into the pain. You can either physically touch the area or hold your hands a little way away from it. Now visualise yourself like a vessel, with the healing energy or light flowing into the top of your head, and down into the flower of your heart centre. From here the energy flows out and down through your arms, out through your hands and so into the person. Mentally ask for the pain to be healed, and then let go of any attachment to the outcome.

Keep your hands in the position until you are aware of the energy lessening, or maybe the heat dissipating (if you felt heat). Never just pull your hands away. Always be aware of what the energy is doing, and if in doubt, check with your inner guidance that you have finished the treatment. It can be really painful to have someone pull away before completion — akin to a surgeon operating, but then leaving the scar unstitched. You will find that the whole process is actually a lot simpler than it sounds, so just let it flow; don't expect miracles straight away and you might be pleasantly surprised.

Remember you are a channel. Do not try to control or manipulate the energy; just trust that whatever is needed will happen even if it may not be what you choose or even what you expect. With pain, you can mentally ask for the healing energy to dissipate the pain, or for the healing to draw the pain out — again, feel into what is the most appropriate method at the time.

If you find it easy to visualise, and you imagine the light talked of earlier coming down through your head and heart and flowing out through your hands, be aware also of the earth energy coming up through your feet (this awareness helps to ground you) until it joins with the light energy in your heart centre. How does this feel for you? Can you be aware of what happens when the two energies meet and flow out through this heart centre?

What happens after you have finished healing? Are you aware of feeling re-charged, or do you feel drained and tired? If the latter is the case, then you haven't been channelling so much as giving of your own energy. Be aware of this next time and remember to allow the healing energy to flow THROUGH you and not from you. The most common occurrence is for the healer to actually feel refreshed — after all, the healing energy is flowing through you so why can't it revitalise you at the same time as the person receiving the healing? Don't be afraid of any reactions which might occur, but allow them to be. Feel the caring for the other person and know that if the light is with you then all else will follow.

If after doing all these exercises you find that life is leading you further along the path towards channelling in a wider sense, open yourself to finding someone with whom you can learn and grow — someone who has both experience and expertise in using the light in as many aspects of channelling as possible. You may like to find someone who specialises in the area you particularly want to work in, but it also helps if you can understand the other areas too. Go on recommendation, but also follow your own gut feeling: you need to feel total trust in the person you choose to work with so that you can let go and let the God energy flow through your being.

Before you proceed too far, it would be as well to read the following chapter so that you become aware of some of the dangers involved, and how there are some unscrupulous people out there ready to take a novice for a complete ride. However, there are also many genuine people who work with the light and can help you gain access to whatever level is right for you. Trust you own inner feelings and you'll be led along whatever path is right for you.

Chapter Nine

Abuse, Misuse and the Hazards Involved

In Chapter 6 I mentioned the dangers involved in playing in unknown areas such as black magic. In this chapter I will go into further detail about how problems can arise, as well as discussing how fragile we are as human beings, and how people's egos can lead them into temptation and so into trouble.

The ego is the 'I' or the self of any person. Someone on an ego trip is using behaviour that is intended to attract attention and admiration for the sake of boosting that individual's own ego. The majority of people who enter into psychic or spiritual realms and end up with problems, are those whose ego has become too controlling, or who have become addicted to the power and cannot stop.

I'll give you an example — an extreme one, but nonetheless true. Many years ago, as a result of a workshop, a particular man whom I shall call Adam learnt to tune in to his inner guidance. He had no trouble at all receiving clear messages, and found healing a delightful and easy tool for helping people feel better. He practised channelling his own inner guidance on a daily basis, and it flowed easily and naturally, but gradually the quality seemed to change. At first the information was loving and accurate, and for himself alone. After a while he was supposedly receiving guidance for others. Although I tried talking to him about what was happening, he felt he knew better, and was flying really high with his new-found power.

A few days later he started telling a group of people exactly what they MUST do, and how he was to be their leader and everyone was to take orders from him. Some people listened; others were discriminating enough to realise that all was not as it should be. Early one morning my husband and I received an emergency phone call: Adam was now totally possessed by a male entity, he was delighting in the sense of power that it brought, and harassing all those in close proximity to him.

After 12 hours of non-stop work, and the release of many

abusive and aggressive entities, Adam became physically violent. Finally he had to be admitted to a private hospital, and for the next few days he was kept sedated. When finally he came round, he was in state of shock and needed considerable care and attention from his family and friends. As a result of that experience, he stayed away from anything to do with the psychic or spiritual for a long time.

What happened was that his ego had found the power that it had long wanted, and he played around with this power. Not listening to anyone else, he actually drew to him beings of darkness filled with negativity and aggression, enjoying their company and revelling in the sense of power. The outcome was not as disastrous as it might have been: cases like this can become candidates for psychiatric institutions and Adam might have had real difficulty in ever reclaiming his sanity. However it was severe enough to be extremely painful for him and for those around him, including his wife and family.

The moral of this is: 'Beware of the ego trap'. Check your motive before you get into this type of work, and keep checking it. If you feel you can save the world, then think again. If you feel you are the answer to everyone else's prayers, then look at what is going on inside you. For no one person has the right to change another, or force another to do his or her will. It is up to each individual to receive inner guidance for him/herself, and to follow it accordingly. To me it's an infringement of my space to have someone force on me: 'This is what my guidance says you must do...'. If anyone says that to you, know immediately that something is wrong, and take steps to change the situation.

In the same way I believe that not only is it unethical for someone to use the trance state to achieve a selfish desire, it's also blatant abuse. It has been known for a trance medium to 'channel' words that involve the client in donating money to the medium, or words that persuade the client to go and work long hours without receiving anything in return, again for the medium concerned or for the medium's organisation.

People who are looking for channelled information from someone else often do so at their own risk. The reason they are looking in the first place might be that they are searching for an easy way out or want to have someone else tell them what to do and how to do it: this way they feel they no longer need to take responsibility for themselves. Some people feel very important to have a 10 000-year-old entity give them information, but they forget that the channelling is only as pure as the source and the channel.

According to some authorities, all channelling is tempered by the mind of the individual through whom it comes. I do agree with this in most cases of conscious mediumship, for what comes through has to be 'translated' from another reality into this one, so obviously the consciousness of the channel has a part to play. However, when someone is in deep trance, with no element of their consciousness present, then I wonder how much of the mind can truly be affecting the information coming through?

Knowledge is a powerful tool in today's society, but knowledge without the wisdom to use it constructively can be very detrimental to the person concerned. Many is the time that I have been aware of huge and specific traumas in my client's past, but have often felt unable — ethically — to share what I am picking up because a) I could be wrong, b) they might not be able to cope with the idea, and c) they might TRY to get in touch with incidents and maybe manufacture what happened, which could be totally counter-productive. I don't believe anyone has the right to force the past or the future onto anyone else. From a therapy standpoint, I am much more comfortable when clients reach the trauma in their own time and at their own pace. (The obvious exception is when triggering someone into a past life that they otherwise might never have been able to get in touch with.)

In essence what I am saying is that unconditional acceptance of channelling can be dangerous. Test it out yourself: do you feel comfortable with what has been said; do you get a positive gut reaction; does it resonate with a deeper part of your being? After all, you would never totally accept all you read in the newspapers, or hear on the radio or television, any more than you would automatically believe everything your friends or business associates tell you. You would think about it first before accepting it as true. As I said in Chapter 1, the important word here is discrimination. Be true to yourself, and trust your own intuition. You *do* know what is best for you and what feels right for you.

I believe that most people who channel are sincere in their belief in what they are doing, and many are doing a fantastic job of bringing wisdom, enlightenment and healing into our physical world. The ones I'm concerned about are those that prey on the gullible and the vulnerable among us, and misuse channelling for their own ends. These include those people who start off with the genuine product and somewhere along the way either their ego or their greed steps in and the whole energy changes.

There are also those members of society who recognise a way to make a quick dollar or two: they advertise some high-sounding being and then charge a fortune for the privilege of being able to hear 'words of wisdom' from this so-called being. Unfortunately channelling has become fashionable in our New Age society, and as a result unscrupulous people are jumping on the band wagon. They fabricate information and other facets of channelling, and so give a bad name to those who are truly allowing the spiritual energy to flow through them for the benefit of mankind.

Recently in Sydney there was an excellent example of this. An unknown medium arrived from the USA and to the accompaniment of much media hype, created a sensation. Said to have toured the States giving his wisdom to many, Carlos (the entity) appeared on many current affairs and daytime television shows through the body of a young Spanish man named Jose Alvarez. I watched the initial show and was horrified by what I saw. For a start the man's transfer into trance was accompanied by much shaking and uncontrollable gyrations that I have never observed with a good medium. Then once he was in trance, he deliberately took a pose that was a complete mimic of Ramtha. From here he proceeded to come across to the interviewer as aggressive: he talked about the usual love and light, but there was none of it apparent in his actions or the way he spoke. It was as if he had no concept of what he was saying — very much a 'Don't do as I do, do as I say' attitude which, coming from a purported Ascended Master, didn't create a valid impression at all!

At the end of that appearance, I felt very angry that such an obvious poser, or possibly even a very low-level entity, could be allowed on national television: it would have put any intelligent person off channelling for good. The following day he hit the newspaper headlines in Sydney by his actions on a daytime television show, where the compere ended up with a glass of water being thrown over him.

A few weeks later a well-respected program, *60 Minutes*, announced that it would prove conclusively that Carlos was a fraud... and they did. In fact Carlos was a deliberate plant, the brain-child of one of the reporters and a sceptic, James Randi, who travels the world proving how easy it is to fool people using illusions and trickery. The words Carlos was speaking were coming straight from Randi, and everything else was an act. In one sense I was pleased — it exonerated those channels who were for real. In other ways I felt really sad — that it was necessary to pull this stunt at all, that a lot of very genuine people had gone to hear Carlos in the Sydney Opera House and had been conned, and that a lot of people would have been totally put off channelling for the rest of their lives. It opened the question once again of validity, and somehow the whole incident left a nasty taste in my mouth.

For those of you who have been fortunate enough to be in contact with those genuinely channelling, do not lose sight of what you felt. There is usually a distinct energy felt and a sense of a particular presence, accompanied by an indescribable and often overwhelming feeling of love. It sometimes brings up feelings of humility and even tears, and at times it is as if the being has even gone beyond the limits of love to a state of total wisdom, a state of simply being. This cannot be apparent with trickery or someone playing games. There have been many instances where research has been carried out, and despite the hoaxes that have been perpetuated, there have been many other cases that have been proven to be totally real and unexplainable.

Some channelled entities have difficulty putting their message across to our level of reality, and many of them are inclined to speak in symbols. These symbols are fine so long as we interpret them correctly, but who is to say which interpretation is the right one? I have often heard forecasts of tidal waves and buildings collapsing, and yet many people believe this to be a totally symbolic message: the wave is seen to be a change of consciousness sweeping over the nation, and the buildings to be people's egos collapsing as a result of the transformation. Yet the fear engendered by such forecasts is still there, and often this fear attracts negativity towards it. This may take the form of a person being drawn towards a similar person, someone who is also filled with this fear. If this person is still trying to work as a channel, and is unable to put his or her own thoughts and beliefs out of the way, the channelling that comes through will not be as pure as it could be.

An obvious misuse of spiritual energy comes from those people who play with the ouija board or hold seances without having the slightest idea of what they are doing — it is not only conscious misuse that leads to trouble. However, there are unscrupulous people (luckily the exception rather than the rule) who recognise a potential medium, and somehow persuade that person to join their group, thus catapulting him or her into extreme danger. Just by using group energy, it is possible to call up spirits when the intention is there, and this is a common way that the unsuspecting and innocent get into a position that is both frightening and difficult to escape from. Many a spirit possession case is a result of people playing in areas they do not understand, or they just do not realise the potential danger of such activities. It is equivalent to handing a box of matches to a toddler and saying: 'Have fun'. The toddler will do everything he or she can with them, including lighting them, and the results are anything but fun.

Having fun and playing is NOT what this area is all about, and many people have learnt this painful lesson the hard way. Tom was a teenager with a strong pull towards the psychic and spiritual, thinking these areas were both exciting and fun to be involved in. Unfortunately he also had a decided inferiority complex, and when the group that he was working with started to channel various entities, he thought it would bring him credibility and popularity to do the same.

The important point here is that he never actually learnt what to do. He just copied what he thought he saw happening, and in time, started to take over the group by trying to run things his way and under his control. To me the strange part about it was that the adults in the group not only let it happen, but actually encouraged him. It took them quite a while to realise that a teenager was not only ill equipped to handle such a situation but was also psychologically unable to do so. The members of the group started to encounter huge problems each time they sat together, to the extent that serious fights developed, healing was no longer taking place, and the entities coming through were all from the dark side.

Eventually the group realised what was happening, and they disbanded. However Tom was still in trouble, and spent many weeks working through a heap of emotional and spiritual problems with both a psychic and a psychiatrist. This is not an act to be copied.

It is easy to understand why Tom went the way he did, but that's not an excuse. If a group is going to sit together for the purpose of attracting or working with any sort of psychic or spiritual energy, then it is vital that there is someone in charge — someone who knows and understands everything that is going on, and who is experienced in dealing with all the different types of situations that can arise. I cannot stress this point enough, for people's sanity may be at stake, and even their lives. It is also important that responsibility is taken, and that those in authority in this field share and teach all that they know, from the basics onwards. This ensures that anyone coming into this area learns how to use the light right from the start, and is aware of the potential dangers involved and how to avoid them.

One of the biggest dangers open to the unsuspecting is that of black magic. In Chapter One I mentioned that energy itself is benign and that it is how energy is used that is important. In others words the same energy can be used for good or for evil. In black magic there is a distinct absence of light — it is misuse of our life energy for the purpose of having power over another being or beings. This means that anyone using energy negatively, such as to harm or destroy, is actually performing a type of black magic.

One of the very early cases of schizophrenia I worked with involved a victim of black magic. She was a young girl who had been travelling overseas, and had met a powerful and charismatic man who wasted no time in gaining control over her. Originally he seduced her, and after that it was easy for him to control her body and mind. He introduced her to the dark side of life, and what she saw and felt over the few months she was under his control left her with almost indelible scars. The amazing part is that she was able to get away and return home at all, and then it took much time and a lot of treatment before she was able to emerge from her psychotic withdrawal into the world. For months everything held terror for her, including her parents, until eventually she started to return to reality and finally was able to live an almost normal life.

One of the areas particularly open to misuse, I believe, is the one in which people are taught to use the power of their minds. That in itself is anything but a crime. However, when the step is taken to learn how to control another's mind, or to draw energy from another living person, then that person has over-stepped the bounds of what is acceptable in society. Although this doesn't really come under the heading of channelling, it is very much a part of the abuse of the New Age movement that is taking place. It is often presented under the auspices of love and light, and yet nothing is further from the truth. To me such misrepresentation is yet another example of blatant misuse of power, and the worrying part of it is that some highly acclaimed people are teaching this, all in the name of self-development.

A case that still leaves me cold when I think about it concerns a young girl, Mary, desperately seeking spiritual learning. Part of this learning centred around her desire to heal, and she found her way to a man who became her guru. Under his guidance she started learning about channelling energy, spiritual practices, and healing. However, after a while with him, she started having weird dreams: it was as if he were sexually invading her body each night, although on the physical level she was totally alone. Becoming really scared, Mary tried to get out of the group that he was teaching, but the reality of the visions increased, leaving her terrified and unrefreshed by sleep each morning. The guru persuaded her not only to stay with the group, but also convinced her that she needed him to teach her, that she was special to him and that she needed to stay with him for further development.

The final straw came when the man coerced her into accompanying him overseas to where he had a 'centre'. She discovered that the place was totally filled with women, all of whom had had similar experiences to her own. Somehow Mary found the strength to resist his mind control sufficiently to leave the place, although she was tormented by the sexual invasion that continued to take place on the non-physical level until she reached out for help. Even then it took much time and effort to counteract the man's powerful coercive energy.

Mary underwent much physical and emotional trauma during this time, and had to look in depth at why she had allowed the whole experience to take place in the first place. Mary was one of the 'lucky' ones: in time she was able to reclaim her own power and control. However there are many others who are still unfortunate enough to be under the control of this power-hungry and unscrupulous person. It sounded to me like the plot for a 'B-grade' movie, but it was only too true, and since then I've come across other similar cases. Invariably it is a situation where someone with power and knowledge tries — for their own selfish purpose — to control someone who is truly searching.

I don't want to put any genuine seekers off the path, but what I do want to do is make you aware of the possibilities for the unwary. When you choose to learn, don't blindly follow just anybody. Use your discrimination: can you trust this person, do you feel really good about him or her at a deep level, does what he/she says ring true to your inner being? Above all, maintain your own sense of self. You are in charge of your own life — it is not for another to take that power away from you. Tune in to your higher self, your divine part, and you will find that answers will be there.

Chapter Ten

Stepping Stones Along the Way

As a result of the constant questions I am asked after lectures and during workshops, I felt it necessary to include a chapter about the experiences and side effects which may be encountered on the way to becoming a channel. Some of these can be peak experiences which you will remember for the rest of your life; others may cause problems which can leave scars for years. The 'norm' falls somewhere between the two however, and most people undergo a mixture of positive and negative events in the process of learning and growing.

One side effect of the growth experience is that we become more open, and therefore more sensitive. It's as if we become finely tuned, and although this opens up a whole new and possibly exciting world, it can also bring a lot of unwanted experiences. It means that we are more aware of what is going on, not only inside ourselves but also inside other people and in the world in general. We become more aware of others' fears and pains, and sensitive to what is happening on a global level as well as on a personal level. It may become difficult to be in large crowds or to go to loud parties, and for many this is the beginning of a totally new lifestyle — as if opening our consciousness means we have to pay more attention to how we live in the world.

Having been very aware of all this for years, I usually take care not to put myself in situations that I can't handle: I no longer go into pubs or bars or places where there is a lot of frenetic or negative energy. If the situation is unavoidable, then I take great pains to protect myself and to close down as far as possible. I managed to get carried away with Christmas shopping last year, however; I ended up at the local markets the Saturday before Christmas, shopping frantically for last-minute presents. So was everyone else, it appeared! After a couple of hours in that environment, I felt so ill that I had to go home: I had forgotten to take any sensible precautions, and my body just couldn't cope. I had to laugh afterwards, for they say you teach best what you most need to learn, and protection is something I always stress as an integral part of the opening-up process.

I know some people who have difficulty living in society at all due to their sensitivity, and this can become a very real problem. I believe our protective strength is like a muscle: it needs much work to build it up, but in time it's possible to face most situations without collapsing from the external pressure. After all, we are physical beings here on earth to learn how to cope with physical reality, so turning our backs on this world isn't going to accomplish anything. It is far better to learn how to deal with whatever causes the difficulties.

Elizabeth Stratton, a healer and counsellor in private practice in New York City, runs workshops in psychic self-defence. As an introduction to one of these workshops she writes: 'The power of psychic energy cannot be overestimated. We are constantly bombarded by the emotions and thoughts of people around us, as well as by the accumulated energies of the environments in which we live and work. We can also be affected by the physical illness of people we are close to, sometimes to the point of acutally manifesting those illnesses as if they were our own'.

One of the real dangers for trainee healers is that they forget to protect themselves before giving a healing. Often students ring up months after learning healing, and describe problems they have suffered as a result of not protecting themselves properly. It may simply be a case of picking up tiredness, but it can be serious too, such as taking on deep emotional or physical pain which in reality belongs to the client.

Some people find that simply the thought of channelling is a frightening proposition, and one that can bring up a lot of emotional issues. Fear of abusing the power is a common issue, as is doubt concerning the authenticity and validity of the channelling: 'What happens if it's only coming from my ego?'. Other common feelings are: 'I'm not worthy enough to channel', or 'It's too big for me to handle'. All these feelings need to be dealt with sensitively and honestly, for they are very real to the person experiencing them, and unfortunately often necessary for that person's growth.

Dr Sandra Gibson, author of the book *Beyond the Mind*,

describes how terrified she was when she first started to encounter psychic experiences over which she had no control. Convinced that she was either going crazy or on the verge of being possessed, she visited a psychologist who reassured her that she was perfectly sane. According to him: 'Being crazy is being unable to function in daily life'. However, he did acknowledge that things were happening in her life that she needed expert help to understand. As a result she went into intensive therapy where she began to understand and embrace the soul part of her, and eventually learnt how to work with it for herself as well as for others.

Eventually Sandra Gibson found herself doing successful readings for friends and clients. However, she was constantly searching for verification. She writes: 'My task was frustrating, for most of my readings dealt with past lives, soul development, and emotional forces at work within the individual, things that are very difficult to verify scientifically'.

She also wanted to determine the source of her guidance and information. 'Was it from my guide, Kirk? Was it from my own soul? From God? Was it from within me or without?' If the information came from within then she was convinced it would be imagination and therefore totally useless. Only if it came from a source outside her did she feel it could be legitimate.

What finally resolved the issue for her was a discussion with her therapist: he told her that her own soul knows everything there is to know, and the difference between within and without is very nebulous on higher levels. This convinced her to look at the value of what she was doing and how it helped the people involved, and so she let go of struggling with these concepts and went on with her rapidly expanding work.

A feeling which is relatively common amongst people developing their channelling skills is that of being over-whelmed: the fear of the responsibility involved can be considerable. To many, this fear is so powerful that, without support and understanding, they turn their backs on the whole spiritual realm and all that it involves.

Over the years I have watched and supported many people moving into the various fields of channelling, and those who had stars in their eyes haven't lasted. It is the ones who have realised, often reluctantly, that it is a part of their make-up and a life path for them, who are able to move through the traumas involved and learn to embrace and use the light.

I want people to realise that channelling is not just a job that can be taken on at random with no thought of the consequences. Obviously, for some it is far less traumatic than for others, depending on the type of childhood they had, their past lives, and their emotional make-up. Often the decision to go into channelling is not a conscious choice however, but something that evolves over time.

When I first started healing in 1974 I was still working as an actress. Without any conscious decision on my part, people started coming to me for healing. Reluctantly at first, due to my feelings of inadequacy and inexperience, I would work with those in need. Gradually, I realised that I was being pushed into this pathway by a force that was both within me and without — a force that was gentle yet powerful. Eventually I gave up the resistance and accepted that this was a part of me, and finally I gave up my acting career and went into healing on a full-time basis. For me this was a natural and comfortable progression, but for some people it can be intensely traumatic.

Elizabeth was having problems during meditation: each time she reached a certain depth, an intense fear would surface, causing her to spontaneously jolt back to reality. In time she realised that another energy was surrounding her body, and so great was her terror that she arrived on my doorstep wondering if she was possessed or going crazy.

In fact neither was the case: she was a very sane human being who had started the opening-up process in a meditation group where no-one had understood what was happening, and she was thus left to cope on her own.

What happened in the session that followed was that I took her back to a past life where she had been a powerful healer. The local priest had approached her and she had tried to help him with his epileptic fits, but there was nothing she could do. As a result he went back to the authorities and told them that she had bewitched him, causing his fits. In those days the penalty for witchcraft was death through fire, and Elizabeth was burnt alive as a witch.

As she died, she vowed that she would never heal again. After all, God had deserted her and had allowed her to be killed, so she would never do His Will again. Having acknowledged this, it was important for Elizabeth to understand why the priest had acted the way he did. Once the understanding was there, she was able to forgive him for wrongly accusing her, and finally she was able to forgive herself for denying God, and so reverse the decision she had made about healing.

Once she had connected with this and released it from her consciousness, she was able to integrate the experience. She came to the realisation that the energy she was resisting in meditation was in fact that utilised for healing. From then on she allowed herself to flow with that energy, and after only a short time Elizabeth became a sensitive and powerful healer.

Another problem that arose as a result of a past life was that concerning Lisa. She had come to see me because she was torn between wanting desperately to heal and do therapy, and the fear it brought up every time she tuned in to someone and 'knew' what was wrong with them: she could see into their minds, and she felt this to be an invasion of their space.

She went back to a lifetime in the latter part of Atlantis when she had been an adept in mind control, and used to draw energy from others for her own ends. These people became zombies as a result of what she did, and Lisa was living with this subconscious knowledge which now prevented her using her power for good purposes. It took quite a considerable time before she was able to forgive herself, as she insisted that she should continue to pay for everything that she had done. However, she finally realised that now she could set the record straight and use the energy for helping people this time around.

Lisa is now an excellent healer and therapist, but over the next few months she had more issues to clear before she was finally able to fully embrace the healing profession. Even now she has times when she doubts if she should really be in this field. These doubts include: 'Am I really good enough', 'Maybe I'm kidding myself' and 'What I'm doing could be dangerous'. These issues arise regularly for people when they first move into the area of healing and need to be sensitively and patiently worked through.

Doubts such as not feeling good enough are very common, and usually stem from childhood issues. These issues can vary from a simple case of not having been a high achiever at school, or never having been good enough to satisfy parents with high expectations, to traumatic events such as an induced birth, or being a victim of assault or sexual abuse.

Tim was continually being told by his father that he wasn't good enough, and what a disappointment he was to his family. If he wasn't among the top three in his class, his father would cane him for not working hard enough. It was hardly surprising therefore, that he should grow up with a large inferiority complex, and much suppressed rage against his father. This rage had to be released before Tim was able to come to terms with what had happened in his childhood. He was then able to move on and embrace life more fully. He started acknowledging his own power and finally he was able to move into the area of healing something he had always wanted to do but had previously been held back by a lack of confidence.

Possibly the most frightening situation I have ever encountered is when someone believes he or she is really going crazy, and no amount of reassurance makes any difference. When they reach this state they are often suicidal, and no amount of talk does any good. The ultimate change has to come from within the person concerned, although strong and loving support is an invaluable aid.

Louise had been on the growth path for some years before she started seeing energies. This, in itself, was hard enough to cope with, but as she became accepting of this, she started feeling the energies within her own body — not just being aware of them like most people, but actually feeling the spin of each energy centre or *chakra* in turn, and staying in the spin. This was followed by all of the centres becoming activated at once, and as each *chakra* spins in the opposite direction to the previous one, it was an uncomfortable and frightening experience for her.

It is hard for anyone who hasn't experienced it to comprehend how terrifying this can be. I have felt this total activation for a brief period of time, and that was bad enough, but to live in it for days at a time made Louise feel she was not only totally out of control, but also that she was going mad. Add to this the impossibility of sleeping during such activity, and you have the picture of someone close to mental breakdown.

In the beginning all we could do was balance the energies as far as was possible, and learn how to move the energy from one centre through and out another centre. Emotional explosions sometimes needed to happen, but there came a time when catharsis was counter-productive and both of us had to be aware of this. Ultimately, we discovered that activation of the individual centres in Louise heralded understanding and new information about that particular centre, information which was subsequently channelled through.

Some time later Louise underwent another crisis period when her life took a new direction, and again the energy became too much for her to cope with. She became aware of the fragility of her human body as opposed to the intensity of the energy contained within it, and wondered how her body could withstand such onslaughts.

Needless to say it did, but accompanied by much pain, trauma, soul-searching, and periods of intense physical activities. One night she ran barefooted for so long that her feet were raw the next day, and yet there was a compulsion to exercise in an attempt to release the energy that seemed to be taking control of her.

Despite all this, Louise underwent experiences that counter-balanced these traumas — peak experiences that left her filled with joy for hours on end; a time when she could 'see' totally what was in front of her despite being heavily blindfolded; confirmation of the material she had channelled from others working in the field, and from researchers who had proven scientifically what she had experienced.

Much of what Louise went through has been classified by Stan and Christina Grof as spiritual emergence experience. Stan Grof has devoted most of his working life to studying non-ordinary states of consciousness. He started his psychoanalytic research as far back as the 'fifties with LSD laboratory studies. He and Christina now concentrate on non-drug intervention techniques to help clients work through and resolve transpersonally related blocks and problems of the psyche. This involves using what they term the 'holotropic' technique, a combination of body work, breathing technique and evocative sound, which in turn can lead to psychic integration, personality growth and increased spiritual awareness.

The Grofs believe that many otherwise healthy individuals are unnecessarily institutionalised, often labelled and treated as schizophrenic, even when not pathologically ill. Many of these people have become disturbed or disoriented by unusual or unexpected psychic disturbances. The symptoms may include emotional distress, perceptual problems and paranormal experiences. The Grofs interpret these as consciousness transformation indicators or spiritual emergence symptoms: Louise's experienced fitted into these parameters.

The Grofs maintain that if this spiritual opening process is properly understood and sympathetically treated as just a difficult stage in a natural process, then positive crisis resolution is possible. The symptoms can arise spontaneously, or they can be the result of various spiritual practices such as *kundalini* arousal techniques, or indeed from any growth work that taps into higher energy or altered states of consciousness. Christina Grof has been instrumental in starting a network of competent personnel who can help people undergoing these spiritual emergence symptoms, and her aim is to see a worldwide network for the support of these people: at the time of writing there are more than 40 of these spiritual emergence networks across the world.

A question often asked is: 'Why do people choose to move into such areas when there can be so many disastrous side effects?' The answer varies from person to person, and I want to stress that people don't all experience the problems I've described in this chapter — they are merely examples of what can happen along the way. There are also overwhelming positive effects, and these usually outweigh the negative ones.

Some people get into the growth field because of an intense desire to discover more about themselves as individuals. Some people have a sense that there is more to life than meets the eye, and they want to discover what that is. More and more people however, are now opening up due to circumstances in their lives: the breakdown of a relationship, the death of a loved one, the discovery of a cancer condition, for example. It's as if each of these events acts as a catalyst for change and, using this event as an opportunity, people start searching: searching for the wholeness and inner peace that is often talked about yet rarely felt. Some go to counsellors or therapists, some go to healers or psychics, while others go to workshops or seminars. What is important is that they start somewhere and continue for as long as they feel is necessary. There are many roads to the same end, and it doesn't matter how that end is achieved, so long as it *is* achieved.

Many people touch into the psychic and spiritual only after intense work in the emotional field: for example, James had been in personal therapy for a while in order to overcome his feelings of powerlessness when in the company of women. In one particular session he touched into the intense trauma that had taken place when, as a very tiny baby, he had been circumcised without anaesthetic (which unfortunately is normal practice). His mother had handed him over to the doctor, and two female nurses had held him down for the brief duration of the operation. His terror and pain had been so great that he had left his body, and this memory of floating in the light came back to him during the session. He felt that he had pleaded with a powerful being of light not to let him come back to the little tortured body, but he had been told that he had much to learn and do. With that he made an abrupt re-entry into his body, discovering the nurses trying to force him to breathe.

After this session, James' attitude underwent a distinct change: he no longer felt powerless around women, and he started becoming more aware of his spirituality. The experience opened his awareness to a 'knowingness' that there is more to life than just what is perceived in the physical reality. He continued his work on the emotional level, but also started exploring spiritual realms and the basics of channelling, which brought him much satisfaction and fulfilment.

The converse also takes place: people start learning about the psychic or spiritual fields, and inevitably they touch into some emotional issue. Robin was convinced he had a new guide with him who was trying to make contact, but he was having a lot of difficulty in receiving any messages. He had been sitting in a spiritual development group for some months, and although his awareness was growing, he felt something was blocking his path.

What the block turned out to be was unresolved grief concerning his father's death, and the so-called guide was none other than his father who had been trying to persuade Robin to release this grief. Although the death had taken place when Robin was a child, it was as if a dam wall had burst as Robin let out tears the child had held back for so long. After that session Robin agreed to do more work on his childhood traumas, and as he freed himself of pain and anger, his abilities in the development group underwent a dramatic improvement. He discovered a natural gift for healing, and the more he cleared himself, the more this gift blossomed. Years later I heard him say: 'The more pain I let go of, the better I felt, and the more I was able to channel this healing energy. This in turn led to me feeling even better, and so I learnt of the exquisite relationship between joy and pain'.

It stands to reason that the more pain a person releases, the better he or she will feel. If this pain comes as a result of the spiritual emergence, it may be a frightening experience, and it may throw up many issues that need resolving. Nevertheless, the end results are invariably positive, provided the situation is handled sensitively by someone with understanding of the process.

An introduction to channelling is not always accompanied by these 'stepping stones', and there are many people working in the field who have never encountered any problems, and have never even heard the term 'spiritual emergence'. However, for those of you who have had to struggle to break through beliefs, conditioning and past traumas, take heart. Ultimately, you will be able to lead a richer, a more rewarding and a more fulfilling life.

CONCLUSION

An important aspect of this book is to understand that channelling can be both a blessing and a source of growth in your life, as well as being a source of pain that needs much support and understanding to work through. However, if you can trust the process and have an experienced support person available at all times, then the hazards are minimised and in time you will be able to move into the joy and leave behind the pain.

In the closing chapter of *Opening to Channel*, the two authors, Sanaya Roman and Duane Packer, write: 'We have watched hundreds of people gain mastery over their lives as they connected with their guides or source selves, awakening to their inner teachers and discovering their abilities to transform themselves and others. We have watched people succeed with their lives, become happier, more prosperous, and discover their life purpose through channelling'.

Many people I know spend time each day tuning in to their inner wisdom and guidance in order that their lives can become more fulfilling and productive. Channelling has become a part of their everyday existence, an integral part without which they would feel empty, incomplete or alone. This tuning in brings wisdom and understanding, calmness and joy, and is a continuous process that, if the person so wishes, remains with that person throughout the whole of his or her life. It is similar to having a constant friend with whom to discuss everything, but without any of the usual demands of friendship; there is a closeness hard to find in a physical relationship, but with none of the battles that often take place.

There is often information coming through that can be totally practical, or words that seem to bring new concepts and understanding into the lives of those who hear it. Whatever form it takes, there is no doubt that channelling can be a strong force for good in one's life, and one that can allow intense opening up to occur on all levels.

Although the path of a channel is rarely smooth, and there are often many stepping stones along the way, the overwhelming majority of people in contact with their divinity within, their higher self, or their guides, would never change that connection. It is something that allows life to be lived to the full with understanding and compassion, and whether this connection is totally for the individual or for the masses is immaterial. What is important is that we, as human beings, become aware of our wholeness, and strive to bring that wholeness into the world in whatever way we are able. If we can utilise the God force or universal energy, and bring this energy into our daily lives, we, as a race, have a chance to expand beyond our five senses, beyond our mind, out into an untapped source of love and healing, for ourselves and for the planet.

* * * * * * * *

Seek and you will find, and whatsoever you find that is pure and of the essence, allow it to flow into you until your whole being is filled with understanding and love. When you are filled with this love energy, then radiate it out to all with whom you come into contact, touching their hearts and minds and spirits. Choose to live life to its fullest, knowing that if your heart is open, all else will fall into its rightful place.

BIBLIOGRAPHY

Brown, R., *Unfinished Symphonies*, Souvenir Press Ltd, London, 1971

Brown, R., *Immortals By My Side*, Bachman and Turner, London, 1974

Caddy, E., *Footprints on the Path*, The Findhorn Foundation, Scotland, 1976

Caddy, E., and McVicar, R., *The Spirit of Findhorn*, The Findhorn Foundation, Scotland, 1977

Chapman, G., and Stemman, R., *Surgeon from Another World*, The Aquarian Press, Northamptonshire, 1978

Coit, L., *Listening: How to Increase Awareness of your Inner Guide*, Swan Publishing, Laguna, California, 1985

Coll, F., *Man and the Universe*, Americana Leadership College, Iowa, 1970

Coll, F., *True Feelings*, Americana Leadership College, Iowa, 1978

Cooke, G., *The New Mediumship*, The White Eagle Publishing Trust, Hampshire, England, 1965

Crum, T., *The Magic of Conflict*, Simon and Schuster, New York, 1987

Dooley, A. (edit), *Guidance from Silver Birch*, Spiritualist Press, London, 1966

Edwards, H., *The Healing Intelligence*, Herbert Jenkins Ltd, London, 1965

Edwards, H., *A Guide to the Understanding and Practice of Spiritual Healing*, The Healer Publishing Co. Ltd, Guildford, England, 1974

Ferrucci, P., *What We May Be*, Jeremy P. Tarcher, Inc., Los Angeles, 1982

Hagon, M., *Journey Within*, The Wentworth Press, Sydney, 1981

Hill, D., *Reaching for the Other Side*, Pan Books, Sydney, 1982

Hill, D., *Edge of Reality*, Pan Books, Sydney, 1987

Hutton, J.B., *Healing Hands*, W.H. Allen, London, 1966

Martin, M., *Hostage to the Devil*, Readers' Digest Press, New York, 1976

Montgomery, R., *A Search for Truth*, Ballantine Books, New York and Toronto, 1966

Polge, C., and Hunter, K., *The Living Image*, Regency Press, London, 1984

Raphael/Carey, K., *The Starseed Transmissions*, Uni-Sun, Kansas City, 1982

Ramala Centre, *The Revelation of Ramala*, Neville Spearman, Jersey, 1978

Regush, Nicholas M., (edit.) *Frontiers of Healing*, Avon Books, New York, 1977

Ritchie, G., *Return from Tomorrow*, Chosen Books, Waco, Texas, 1978

Roberts, J., *Seth Speaks*, Prentice-Hall, Englewood Cliffs, New Jersey, 1972

Roman, S., and Packer, D., *Opening To Channel*, H.J. Kramer Inc., Tiburon, California, 1987

Schucman, Dr H., *The Course in Miracles*, Foundation for Inner Peace, California, 1975

Stokes, D., *Voices in my Ear*, Futura Publications, London, 1980

Street, Rev. N., *Pathway to Spiritual Healing*, CSA Press, Georgia, 1965

Sugrue, T., *There is a River*, Dell, New York, 1942

Swain, J., *On the Death of my Son*, Turnstone Press, Wellingborough, Northamptonshire, 1974

Tebecis, Dr., *Mahikari*, Yoko Shuppansha, Tokyo, 1982

Watson, A., and Drury, N., *Healing Music*, Nature & Health Books, Sydney, and Prism Press, Dorset, 1987

Wavell, S., *Trances*, Allen & Unwin, London, 1966

Wickland, Carl A., *30 Years Among The Dead*, Newcastle Publishing Co. Inc., Los Angeles 1974